...uculty Institute

College
Access:
Opportunity
or
Privilege?

Michael S. McPherson and
Morton Owen Schapiro, Editors

The College Board
New York, NY

The College Board: Connecting Students to College Success

The College Board is a not-for-profit membership association whose mission is to connect students to college success and opportunity. Founded in 1900, the association is composed of more than 5,000 schools, colleges, universities, and other educational organizations. Each year, the College Board serves seven million students and their parents, 23,000 high schools, and 3,500 colleges through major programs and services in college admissions, guidance, assessment, financial aid, enrollment, and teaching and learning. Among its best-known programs are the SAT®, the PSAT/NMSQT®, and the Advanced Placement Program® (AP®). The College Board is committed to the principles of excellence and equity, and that commitment is embodied in all of its programs, services, activities, and concerns.

In all of its book publishing activities the College Board endeavors to present the works of authors who are well qualified to write with authority on the subject at hand and to present accurate and timely information. However, the opinions, interpretations, and conclusions of the authors are their own and do not necessarily represent those of the College Board; nothing contained herein should be assumed to represent an official position of the College Board or any of its members.

Copies of this book are available from your local bookseller or may be ordered from College Board Publications, 45 Columbus Ave., New York, NY 10023. The price is $18.95.

Editorial inquiries concerning this book should be directed to The College Board, 45 Columbus Avenue, New York, New York 10023-6992.

© 2006 The College Board. College Board, Advanced Placement Program, AP, SAT, and the acorn logo are registered trademarks of the College Board. connect to college success is a trademark owned by the College Board. PSAT/NMSQT is a registered trademark of the College Board and National Merit Scholarship Corporation. All other programs and services may be trademarks of their respective owners. Visit the College Board on the Web: www.collegeboard.com.

Library of Congress Cataloging-in-Publication Data

College access : opportunity or privilege? / Michael S. McPherson and Morton Owen Schapiro, editors. 1st ed.
   p. cm.
Includes bibliographical references and index.
ISBN-13: 978-0-87447-774-0
ISBN-10: 0-87447-774-3
1. College costs—United States. 2. Low-income college students—United States.
3. Universities and colleges—United States—Admission. 4. Student aid—United States. I. McPherson, Michael S. II. Schapiro, Morton Owen.

LB2342.C595 2006
378.1'9826942—dc22

2006024115

ISBN-13: 978-0-87447-774-0
ISBN-10: 0-87447-774-3

Printed in the United States of America.
Distributed by Holtzbrinck Publishers, Inc.

"Do what you can,
with what you have,
where you are."

—*Theodore Roosevelt*

College Access: Opportunity or Privilege?
Michael S. McPherson and Morton Owen Schapiro, Editors

Contents

Introduction

Michael S. McPherson and Morton Owen Schapiro

Concerns about college opportunity in America, including a special concern about the low numbers of students from disadvantaged backgrounds at leading public and private universities, seem to be on the rise. Attention has been drawn to these problems through, among other avenues, statements and speeches from influential college and university presidents, innovative outreach programs at some major public universities, and perhaps especially the publication of William Bowen, Martin Kurzweil, and Eugene Tobin's important book, *Equity and Excellence in American Higher Education*.[1]

In this volume, we present a set of research and policy studies designed to illuminate the various dimensions of this important problem. This introductory essay has two purposes: to provide readers with an overview of the essays presented here, and to place the issues of inequality in postsecondary education in the United States into the larger context of educational and social inequality against which these higher education issues play out.

To gain a comprehensive view of the problems of limited representation of students from low-income backgrounds and of first-generation college students in American higher education, it is necessary to look at these issues through different lenses, ranging from a close-up of the challenges as they confront individual colleges and universities, to broader questions of policy and practice for American higher education as a whole, and finally to still broader questions concerning the background conditions that shape the experiences and opportunities for students from different social classes beginning at their earliest age. We need to be clear in distinguishing options and actions that are available to individual colleges and universities from broader issues of public policy and collective action that can only be undertaken at broader levels.

Overview

It is useful at the outset to sketch a broad overview of economic diversity in America's postsecondary universe. As is well known, children from poor families and from families where neither parent attended college are less likely to finish high school and, among those who do graduate from high school, are less likely

---

1. University of Virginia Press, 2005.

to go on to college. Figures 1 and 2 summarize evidence on high school dropout rates and college enrollment rates for different income groups over time. Among those who do enroll in a postsecondary institution, children from disadvantaged backgrounds are disproportionately likely to enroll in public community colleges,

Figure 1. High school dropout rates by family income, 1975–2000

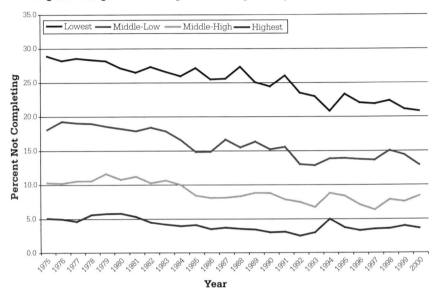

Figure 2. College enrollment rate of high school graduates by income, 1975–2003

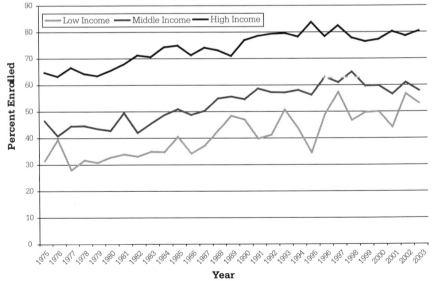

Source: *Digest of Education Statistics 2003*, Table 108. http://nces.ed.gov/programs/digest/d03/tables/dt108.asp

a starting point from which prospects for ultimately earning a bachelor's degree are low. They are far less likely than other students to enter highly selective colleges and universities. As Table 1 shows, in 1999 fewer than 6 percent of freshmen from low- and middle-income families (less than $60,000) attended highly selective colleges, while more than a quarter of those from families with incomes over $200,000 did.

A key factor helping to explain these results is the high correlation between income and standardized test scores in the United States. By no means does this score difference explain all the variation among income groups in college access and attainment: Even among high test-scoring youth, those with low incomes are less likely to go on to college, as indicated in Table 2. Among students in the highest income

Table 1. Distribution of first-time, full-time freshmen by income and institutional selectivity, fall 1999 (Income in the thousands)

1999	<$20	$20–$30	$30–$60	$60–$100	$100–$200	>$200	All Groups
2-yr public	39.0%	38.8%	35.5%	29.8%	16.8%	10.1%	30.9%
2-yr private	3.7%	2.7%	2.4%	1.8%	2.2%	3.5%	2.4%
Low Select 4-yr	41.9%	41.8%	41.8%	42.4%	42.0%	35.4%	41.7%
Medium Select 4-yr	9.7%	11.5%	14.9%	18.0%	23.1%	25.6%	16.5%
High Select 4-yr	5.8%	5.2%	5.4%	8.0%	16.0%	25.5%	8.5%
	100.0%	100.0%	100.0%	100.0%	100.0%	100.0%	100.0%

Source: *The American Freshman, 1999.* Cooperative Institutional Research Program, University of California–Los Angeles, 1999.

Table 2. Postsecondary enrollment rates of 1992 high school graduates by family income and math test scores

Math Test Scores	Lowest Income	Second Quartile	Third Quartile	Highest Income
All				
Lowest Third	48	50	64	73
Middle Third	67	75	83	89
Top Third	82	90	95	96
Four-year				
Lowest Third	15	14	21	27
Middle Third	33	37	47	59
Top Third	68	69	78	84
Two-Year				
Lowest Third	33	36	43	46
Middle Third	34	38	36	30
Top Third	14	21	17	12

Source: Sandy Baum and Kathleen Payea, *Education Pays 2004*, The College Board, p. 30

quartile, fewer than 1 in 20 high-scoring students fail to enroll in college immediately after high school. For high-scoring students in the bottom income quartile, about 18 percent fail to do so. Nonetheless, young people from disadvantaged economic backgrounds clearly have substantially lower test scores and high school grades, and these facts are a major reason for their lower levels of high school completion and postsecondary participation and success. Table 3 displays the strong and persistent relationship between family income and scores on the SAT®.

Standardized tests come in for a lot of criticism, much of it deserved, but it is important not to be too hasty in dismissing the message that these score differences—as well as differences in high school academic performance—bring. That unwelcome message is this: Educational opportunity in the United States is simply spectacularly unequal. For reasons most people could easily name, students from impoverished backgrounds are less well educated and less well prepared for college than are those from more favored backgrounds. There is no reason to believe that there is anything inherently wrong with these kids—this is not a matter of genetics. Rather, the simple fact is that they have grown up and been educated in circumstances that are much less favorable than those facing other Americans. These important features of American education are part of the background against which the policies and practices of a given college or university are set.

Acting alone, there are insurmountable limits to what one college or university can do to influence these basic background conditions. These circumstances thus do much to shape the problem individual universities and colleges confront when thinking about how to make their campuses more economically diverse. How that problem "presents" itself depends very much on where the particular college

Table 3. SAT (total) score averages, by family income, selected years

Family Income	95–96	97–98	99–00	2002–03
less than $10,000	873	873	872	864
$10,000–$19,999	920	914	907	889
$20,000–$29,999	964	959	949	927
$30,000–$39,999	992	992	983	964
$40,000–$49,999	1016	1015	1008	993
$50,000–$59,999	1034	1032	1026	1012
$60,000–$69,999	1049	1046	1039	1025
$70,000–$79,999	1064	1059	1054	1041
$80,000–$100,000	1085	1085	1079	1065
more than $100,000	1129	1131	1129	1123

Source: *Digest of Education Statistics 2003*, Table 133.
Note: SAT scores are recentered.
http://nces.ed.gov/programs/digest/d03/tables/dt133.asp

or university in question is located in the higher education landscape. Thus, for example, for the great majority of private colleges and universities, finding enough poor kids who can meet the admissions standards is not the problem. Indeed, although it is not widely understood, the majority of the more than 1,500 private nonprofit colleges and universities in this country are essentially "open admission" to anyone with a high school diploma. They are (nearly) open admission, that is, from an academic point of view. They are not open admission, however, from a financial point of view.

Most private colleges ration access to their campuses according to ability to pay. Many do this directly by rejecting some "high financial need" applicants, while accepting other "low or no need" applicants with weaker academic qualifications. Others do so less directly by admitting high need applicants but denying them adequate financial aid to attend.[2] These simple truths do not reflect any lack of moral fiber among the leaders of these colleges: They simply reflect the fact that a college, in order to continue to operate, has to pay the bills. Only a relative handful of private colleges and universities can afford to admit the freshman class without regard to family financial capacity and at the same time meet the financial needs of all those admitted students who choose to enroll.

Let us make this more concrete. Suppose you were to make a trip to the next annual meeting of the American Council on Education and ask the first three private college presidents you ran into to name the biggest problem their institutions face regarding the admission of low-income students. The odds are very good that (in the absence of microphones) all three would say: The problem with low-income students is that there are simply too many of them. They would love to trade in some of their low-income students for some full-pay students who can help pay the bills. Indeed, the reality is that even many nationally ranked and highly selective private universities and colleges would stagger under the burden if they succeeded in enrolling many more low-income students. Our essay in this volume documents how the awarding of financial aid grants to students varies with both their academic background and their ability to pay and shows that over time aid, especially at private colleges, has become more generous to students from higher-income families, as colleges try to leverage their financial aid dollars to recruit more students who can help pay the bills.

The situation in public higher education is not so different as one might think. The University of North Carolina at Chapel Hill, for example, has recently announced an ambitious—and laudable—program to increase its representation of low-income

---

2. See Michael S. McPherson and Morton Owen Schapiro, *The Student Aid Game: Meeting Need and Rewarding Talent in American Higher Education* (Princeton, N.J.: Princeton University Press, 1998).

students. This program, called the Carolina Covenant, eliminates loans from the financial aid packages for all students from families with incomes at or below 200 percent of the federal poverty level. It is accompanied by serious communication and recruitment efforts targeted at students from low-income and first-generation college families. David Breneman's essay in this volume describes that program and reports on UNC's Provost Robert Shelton's assessment of its challenges and potential.

This fine initiative provokes an intriguing question: Why is it that Chapel Hill can do this, while the other public universities and colleges in North Carolina either can't or won't? The short, simple answer is that Chapel Hill can do this because it has so many *fewer* low-income students than other public colleges and universities in North Carolina. Those low numbers of low-income students trace back in turn to the fact that UNC-Chapel Hill has a high level of admissions selectivity and, as we discussed earlier, the very strong relationship between family income and precollege academic achievement implies that relatively few low-income students will be able to satisfy the admissions requirements of a top-ranked public university. Conversely, other less-selective North Carolina public institutions have so many low-income students that they couldn't afford to eliminate loans for all of them. The phenomenon described here for North Carolina applies to many other states as well. The "flagship" public institutions typically have an affluent student clientele—sometimes with higher average family incomes than the student bodies at private institutions in the same state— as a result both of higher academic standards and higher costs of attendance for families (if only because of the need to live away from home).

There is a real irony here: The colleges, both public and private, that are currently making the most visible efforts, and getting the most public attention, for expanding their low-income student populations educate many fewer low-income students than do a great many other colleges and universities that don't get a lot of credit for their efforts.

Issues Facing Highly Selective Colleges and Universities

An obvious lesson from this overview is that in thinking about the options available to institutions it is extremely important not to overgeneralize. The differences in circumstances of individual colleges and universities are spectacularly large, both within and between the public and private sectors. Whether one thinks in terms of educational mission, available resources, or character of the students served, it would be hard to exaggerate the variation in the American postsecondary education scene. Policies that make sense in one part of this universe may be infeasible, or even sometimes perverse, elsewhere.

Moreover, outside of a small, charmed circle of "elite" institutions in both public and private higher education, money is a dominant factor in how policies toward disadvantaged students are shaped. A well-established moral principle is that "ought implies can": One cannot be morally required to do something it is not in one's power to do. For many colleges and universities, what they are able to do regarding disadvantaged students is severely limited by their resources. Finally, of course, even the wealthiest universities are constrained by the background conditions discussed above, notably the strong positive relationship between family income and students' level of academic preparation for college.

From all that has been said so far, it might appear that we think that what Harvard or Wellesley or the University of Virginia does regarding students from poor families is of little consequence—a kind of sideshow. These "elite" institutions are merely a drop in the bucket. This would be a serious misreading of what we intend to convey.

It is indeed true that in sheer head-count terms, the set of private colleges and universities who can strive to increase substantially their enrollment of low-income students without serious worry about the financial impact of aiding them is quite small, arguably not even including all the Ivy League universities. Indeed, there are colleges and universities ranked in the top 20 by *U.S. News & World Report* who are not need-blind—that is, who currently turn down some applicants in favor of others with weaker qualifications who can pay more. As Breneman reports in his essay, Henry Bienen, president of Northwestern University, is clear in acknowledging the many competing demands on the resources of a leading private university, even as Sylvia Manning, chancellor of the University of Illinois at Chicago (UIC), emphasizes the severe fiscal pressures endured by a rising urban institution like UIC in competing with more established institutions for resources, for students, and for faculty.

In public higher education, the number of universities with discretionary resources to apply to helping finance the education of a larger number of high-need students is likewise limited: It's likely, for example, that only one or two universities in the Big Ten could command the resources to undertake a program as generous as the Carolina Covenant described above.

Nonetheless, it would be a huge mistake to dismiss the policies of these leading institutions as being of minor importance. William G. Bowen's essay in this volume makes a powerful case for the unique importance of this set of institutions and the special significance for our society of expanding their enrollment of disadvantaged students—points reinforced by Amherst President Anthony Marx's comments as reported by Breneman. Graduates of these colleges and universities disproportionately occupy leadership roles in our society.

To cite some obvious but striking numbers, soon we will have experienced 20 consecutive years of presidents who hold a degree from Yale University. Since Ronald Reagan, every major party presidential candidate has held a degree from Harvard or Yale. Both the undergraduate and graduate backgrounds of the current Supreme Court justices show a similar predominance of training from highly selective institutions, and most of the justices of the federal circuit courts have similar origins. Increasing the numbers of students from disadvantaged backgrounds who attend these elite institutions will not only raise the likelihood of people with such backgrounds winding up in such leadership roles, but it will also broaden the experience of all those who attend such institutions. Both seem clearly desirable outcomes in a democratic society.

Moreover, these colleges and universities themselves play a prominent leadership role in American higher education. By visibly committing their own efforts to the cause of achieving more economic diversity in their student bodies, these institutions may have influence on the broader public policy dimensions of this problem, which we discuss briefly below. And, of course, these affluent universities and colleges have the resources and hence the obligation (here the principle is "Can implies should!") to make the effort. Moreover, as Hill and Winston show in their essay in this volume, there is good reason to believe that the pool of well-qualified, low-income applicants is more than sufficient to permit highly selective colleges and universities to expand their enrollment of disadvantaged students. We therefore fully endorse the Bowen-Kurzweil-Tobin arguments reviewed and amplified in Bowen's essay advocating that these leading universities should "put a thumb on the scale" in favor of admitting (and aiding) more low-income and first-generation college students, as well as strengthening their outreach and communication efforts toward such students.

We agree as well with Bowen's assertion that "affirmation action" for economically disadvantaged students cannot substitute for race-based affirmative action. Although blacks and Hispanics are disproportionately likely to be poor, the fact is that poor whites still substantially outnumber poor members of minority groups. Replacing race-based affirmative action with socioeconomically based affirmative action would drastically reduce the representation of racial minorities at leading colleges and universities. Justice O'Connor speculated in her decision in *Grutter v. Bollinger* that the need for race-based affirmative action would fade away within the next 25 years. In their essay in this volume, Jesse Rothstein and his colleagues subject this guess to careful empirical scrutiny and find little reason for optimism.

These, then, are important efforts deserving of attention and support, but we must also recognize the limitations of policies for greater enrollment of disadvantaged students at highly selective public and private institutions (as Bowen and his colleagues clearly do). First, this group of colleges and universities really are a sliver of American postsecondary education, representing perhaps 2 percent or less of all freshmen. Second, more aggressive admissions and recruitment policies at leading places will probably add, on net, very few students to higher education. In elite private higher education, almost all students who apply to the top places also apply to "safety" schools. Think about what will happen if Harvard or Swarthmore admits somewhat more students from low-income families, while turning down some more affluent students to make room in the class. Those low-income students will be students who otherwise would have attended (and received aid at), say, Syracuse or Lafayette. Meanwhile those newly rejected high-income students will now wind up at Syracuse or Lafayette or comparable schools. This is a good trade for all the colleges involved—Harvard and Swarthmore get the greater economic diversity they seek while Lafayette and Syracuse get the increment in full-pay students that they need—and it is very likely good for society as well, but it does not expand the number of low-income or first-generation college students who wind up in college.

In public higher education, there may be more reason to expect some increase in the total enrollment of disadvantaged students as a result of aggressive recruitment and aid programs, which may encourage some students to think about college who otherwise wouldn't. This is especially likely to hold true when there is a focus on disadvantaged rural areas that lack a broad range of local postsecondary education options. Even here, though, much of the activity is likely to be the movement of students from community colleges or less prestigious publics to leading institutions, especially when, as in North Carolina and Virginia, the universities are offering the same attractive options to out-of-state as to in-state, low-income students. The essay in this volume by Sarah Turner and Jeffrey Tebbs reports early findings from an ongoing study of the University of Virginia's efforts to mount an aggressive outreach and student aid program for disadvantaged students.

Issues Facing Postsecondary Education As a Whole

It is time now to pull the focus back from the highly selective colleges and universities to the broader landscape of postsecondary education. Two points immediately become clear. First, it is here, outside the "elite" sector, where a lot of the low-income students who do go on to college actually enroll. Although there is a tremendous variation among institutions, there is a good deal of economic diversity within the student populations of many community colleges, nonflagship public four-year colleges and universities, and the less selective private colleges and universities. Second, money is a big issue at these places in ways that go beyond the issue of capacity to admit low-income students that we have already discussed. Many students in both public and private higher education are under considerable financial strain, with heavy loans, the burden of work while in school, the expectation to contribute resources to meet family needs, and so on. These burdens may not only discourage enrollment; they are also likely to interfere with learning and success in college. Finally, the weak financial condition of many of the institutions that disadvantaged students attend may impair their educational effectiveness as a result of large classes, heavy reliance on part-time faculty, difficulties in offering courses in proper sequence, lack of academic counseling, and so on. Alfredo de los Santos, Jr. emphasizes these points in his analysis of the plight of America's community colleges, reported by Breneman. One way of looking at this point is as follows: One aspect of improving education for disadvantaged students is to encourage the movement of those who are well qualified to more affluent and successful institutions. A second aspect is to improve the quality of the instruction offered at the places where disadvantaged students are currently enrolled. Looked at from a systemwide point of view, these two strategies need not be alternatives, and both clearly are worth undertaking.

The difficulties in funding both disadvantaged students and the institutions they attend raise important public policy questions about the degree to which our society is actually willing to invest in the postsecondary education of students from impoverished backgrounds. Although there has been much attention to the large percentage increases in public tuition in recent years, there has been less emphasis on a major contributing cause of those tuition increases: a substantial reduction in the share of public higher education revenues supplied by state governments, as state budgets have been squeezed and Medicaid costs have skyrocketed. Indeed, the impression that the costs of public higher education are "skyrocketing" out of control depends on focusing only on tuition increases, while ignoring what has been happening to government support for public higher education. As Table 4 shows, rates of growth in spending on public higher education (combining that by governments and by families) have roughly paralleled rates of growth in GDP, whether viewed on an aggregate or on a per capita basis, through the whole period from 1980 to 2000. Indeed, in the 1990s, spending actually grew more slowly than GDP. Such an allocation of national resources to public higher education seems an odd and disturbing choice in light of the

Table 4. Comparative real growth rates in public higher education costs and GDP

Period	Annual Growth Rates	
	Public Higher Ed	**GDP**
A. Public Higher Education Spending Per Student Compared to GDP Per Capita		
1980-81 to 1990-91	1.92%	2.07%
1990-91 to 1999–2000	2.25%	2.13%
B. Aggregate Public Higher Education Spending Compared to GDP		
1980-81 to 1990-91	3.14%	3.04%
1990-91 to 1999–2000	2.95%	3.38%

Note: "Education costs" are measured as education revenues less revenues from auxiliary enterprises and student aid.
Sources: Educational costs and enrollments: *Digest of Educational Statistics 2002*; GDP and Population: *Economic Report of the President 2003*.

importance of higher education in the world. Weakening government support for public higher education coupled with an increasing burden on families to pay tuition is likely to be especially consequential for low-income students, who for obvious reasons are more vulnerable to shifts in public support than are their more affluent counterparts.

Institution-level policies are clearly important for the broad range of less selective colleges and universities that serve large number of disadvantaged students. There are legitimate questions about ways they could manage their resources more effectively and perhaps especially about ways to improve their prospects for successful program completion by disadvantaged students who attend these institutions. The essay in this volume by Michael Kirst and his colleagues reviews a number of issues that influence the capacity of disadvantaged high school students to accomplish a successful transition to higher education. Yet limitations on discretionary resources at many of these institutions cause issues about public policy to loom large. There are difficult questions to be faced about how best to allocate resources within the public higher education system, between for example community colleges and four-year public institutions. There are also important and difficult questions about developing mechanisms for delivering public subsidies more effectively to encourage both enrollment and program completion for disadvantaged students. Although there are challenges aplenty here for economists and other public policy analysts, an important challenge is one of political will. There is little doubt that, with broad public support, policies could be crafted that would direct both state and federal resources effectively toward expanding educational opportunity for disadvantaged students at the college level. Whether such policies can find widespread political support is, however, not clear.

Getting disadvantaged students into college is plainly not enough—success in learning and in earning degrees is also vital. Although most of the emphasis in this volume is on issues concerning initial entry to college, problems of persistence and completion are also of major importance. Breneman reports on remarks by Nancy Vickers, president of Bryn Mawr, concerning cultural and social difficulties sometimes faced by disadvantaged students at schools where they are outnumbered by more affluent colleagues. In their essay, Mike Nettles and Catherine Millett of the Educational Testing Service present evidence from a recent quantitative study of factors influencing persistence in college.

The Larger Picture of Educational Opportunity

We must now enlarge our perspective once again to consider the society-wide issue of precollegiate education and especially the strong correlation between income and levels of academic preparation for college. As we have seen, it is this basic set of relationships that structures the problem of opportunity both for elite colleges and universities and for postsecondary education as a whole. We know that the gaps in academic performance between more- and less-advantaged children begin very early—in fact before kindergarten—and grow and persist through high school.

Thanks to the standards movement in elementary and secondary education and to the No Child Left Behind (NCLB) Act of 2001, this nation is focusing attention on this problem of achievement gaps more clearly than perhaps it has ever done before. If nothing else, the requirement in NCLB to report the comparative test performances of different subgroups of the school population makes it impossible for school systems to "average the problem away." Plainly an important dimension of this problem is to learn how to improve schools—and the entire education system—in ways that will address these achievement gaps. The challenge here encompasses questions about instructional effectiveness, the effectiveness of school and school system organization, and the financing of education. NCLB's contribution is to shine a spotlight on the issue and to punish school systems that don't improve, but publicity and sanctions will have limited effectiveness in the absence of knowledge about how to improve.[3]

In addition, while we certainly want schools to do all they can to close these achievement gaps (through improving the performance of those who do poorly),

---

3. The case for research on how to improve instruction is well made in Stephen W. Raudenbush, "Learning from Attempts to Improve Schooling: The Contribution of Methodological Diversity," *Educational Researcher*, 34, No. 5 (2005): 25–31.

we must recognize that the schools are highly unlikely to be able to accomplish this work by themselves. Children born into impoverished families and impoverished communities face severe developmental challenges—in health care, in the home environment (time for parental attention, availability of books, a quiet place to study, etc.), and in the community environment (presence of role models, safety and security, worthwhile out of school opportunities, etc.).

Moreover, we have also as a nation permitted the extent of inequality in wealth and income to rise, and have done little to reduce the incidence of child poverty even as the nation's wealth has grown dramatically. The causes of changes in wealth distribution are complex and far from fully understood, but they certainly include deliberate choices in government policy such as changes in the tax system that favor the wealthy and cutbacks in government programs that are important to the poor. Unless we as a nation are willing to face up to these underlying conditions, we are asking our schools—and the disadvantaged children who attend them—to overcome very steep odds. Some of these schools and students manage to overcome the odds and we should strive to help more to do so. But we cannot simply leave this challenge to the schools (and still less to the colleges who have limited capacity to compensate for inequalities in preparation that are 18 years in the making). When one takes this wide-angle view of the problems of educational inequality in the United States, it becomes apparent that health policy, housing policy, and tax policy are inseparable from education policy.

⊞ ⊞ ⊞ ⊞

There is one final challenge to acknowledge. Suppose we were to succeed in substantially raising the academic preparation of disadvantaged students and in moving significantly toward closing the achievement gaps. Then as a society we would be faced with a good many more students from low-income families ready and eager to attend college and complete four-year degrees. As things stand now, the evidence is that we as a society would be unwilling to pay those bills. It would indeed be tragic if No Child Left Behind succeeded in grade schools and high schools only so that we could leave these children behind at the college door.

Section I:

"A Thumb on the Scale"

Extending Opportunity:
"What Is to Be Done?"[1]

William G. Bowen

This essay outlines what I see as important tasks ahead for those of us who believe that education should be an important engine of opportunity in America. In the last 40 years, progress—significant progress—has been made in opening up opportunity, but barriers aplenty remain, including barriers related to race and socioeconomic status. (I leave to other, more courageous, souls the topics of gender and religion, thinking of Harvard and Columbia.)

Race in America

Race remains the most deep-seated and intransigent barrier to opportunity. As Ronald Dworkin has put it, "The worst of the stereotypes, suspicions, fears, and hatreds that still poison America are color-coded."[2] That was, is, and will remain the reality in this country for the foreseeable future.[3] I was recently asked about the prospects for race-based affirmative action in higher education in light of the Supreme Court decisions in the University of Michigan cases.[4] My one-word answer was "Bright." I am bemused by speculations to the contrary in articles with titles such as "Michigan: Who Really Won?"[5]

Taken together, the *Grutter* and *Gratz* decisions tell us these things about the legal status of race-based affirmative action in the United States:

(1) In the words of Sandra Day O'Connor's opinion in *Grutter*: "Today we hold that the [University of Michigan] Law School has a compelling interest in attaining a diverse student body...

---

1. With apologies to Vladimir Lenin, who gave this title to his famous 1902 pamphlet in which he argued that "while capitalism predisposes the workers to the acceptance of socialism, it does not spontaneously make them conscious Socialists." (See Marxists Internet Archive, http://www.marxists.org.)

2. Ronald Dworkin, "Affirming Affirmative Action," *New York Review of Books* 45, No. 16 (October 22, 1998): 99–100.

3. For an exceptionally clear-headed examination of why this is true, see Glenn C. Loury, *The Anatomy of Racial Inequality* (Cambridge, Mass.: Harvard University Press, 2002).

4. This part of my remarks draws heavily on a talk I gave at a University of Michigan symposium, April 14, 2005.

5. Jeffrey Selingo, "Michigan: Who Really Won?" *Chronicle of Higher Education* (January 14, 2005). For a far less equivocal position, see Roger Clegg, "Time Has Not Favored Racial Preferences," *The Chronicle Review* (January 14, 2005).

The Equal Protection Clause does not prohibit the use of race in admissions decisions to further a compelling interest in obtaining the educational benefits that flow from a diverse student body."[6]

(2) At the same time, in rejecting the admissions policy used by the undergraduate College of Literature, Science, and the Arts, *Gratz* makes clear that the use of mechanical approaches such as "bonus points" for being from an underrepresented minority group is not permitted; schools must consider all candidates on an "individualized" basis.

Having always believed strongly in the nuanced consideration of each candidate, this outcome seems just right to me. I believe that individualized approaches to admissions decisions are both better on the merits and much more defensible politically.

The power of the majority opinion in *Grutter* was summarized well by Linda Greenhouse: "The result of today's rulings was that Justice Powell's solitary view that there was a 'compelling state interest' in racial diversity, a position that had appeared undermined by the Court's subsequent equal protection rulings in other contexts and that some lower federal courts had boldly repudiated, has now been endorsed by five justices and placed on a stronger footing than ever before."[7]

This "stronger footing" reflects two principal conclusions stated emphatically in the majority opinion in *Grutter*. First, the Court dramatically expanded the rationale for enrolling a diverse class to include not only the on-campus educational benefits of diversity but also the preparation of larger numbers of well-educated minority candidates for leadership positions in the professions, business, academia, the military, and the government. "Democratic legitimacy" is introduced as one of the principal societal needs that race-sensitive admissions addresses, and an extraordinary coalition of *amici* argued—eloquently—for this rationale. Second, the Court was clear that "narrow tailoring does not require exhaustion of every conceivable race-neutral alternative." The claim that there exist race-neutral means to obtain the educational benefits of diversity was greeted with a high degree of skepticism if not outright disbelief.

Against this backdrop, what are we to make of the evidence of declines in minority enrollment at certain schools in the aftermath of the Supreme Court decisions—in the undergraduate programs at the University of Michigan and

---

6. Quoted in William G. Bowen, Martin A. Kurzweil, and Eugene M. Tobin, *Equity and Excellence in American Higher Education* (Charlottesville, Va.: University of Virginia Press, 2005), 148. Much of the rest of this part of my remarks is based on Chapter 6 of this book.

7. Linda Greenhouse, "The Supreme Court: Affirmative Action: Justices Back Affirmative Action by 5 to 4, but Wider Vote Bans a Racial Point System," *New York Times* (June 24, 2003): A1.

Ohio State, for example? My answer: Not much. Should it surprise anyone that elimination of bonus points for minority group membership and addition of essay requirements apparently discouraged some minority applicants from applying? Of course not. For minority candidates, the cost-benefit ratio of applying changed fairly significantly. Moreover, the enrollment data collected by the *Chronicle* for 29 colleges with competitive admissions found that minority enrollment declined at only 7 of them; it increased at 11 and was mixed or ambiguous at the other 11. Longer term, there is no reason why minority enrollments at most places should not increase. And preliminary data for the class that entered in the fall of 2005 suggest that minority enrollments will in fact rebound at schools such as the University of Illinois at Urbana-Champaign, the University of Michigan, and the University of Georgia.[8]

So, the first thing that I believe we should do, looking ahead, is to reemphasize to one and all that race-sensitive admissions policies are on a firmer legal footing than ever before and should be actively promoted, not just defended. At the same time, we should of course do all we can to hasten the day, even if it proves to be more than 25 years from now, when race-sensitive policies will not be needed.

The second thing that we should do is listen to what the Court said, heed the principles that the Court established, and give careful consideration to modifying "enrichment" and other programs that were racially exclusive to eliminate the exclusivity without harming—and sometimes even strengthening—the ability of such programs to achieve their purposes. This approach is both sensible and practical, as I believe the Mellon Foundation's experience with what is now called "The Mellon Minority Undergraduate Fellowship (MMUF) Program" demonstrates. I regard the modifications that were made in MMUF and in MIT's exceptionally well-regarded summer program, to mention only those two, as "aggressively thoughtful" responses to a changed legal environment. From all indications, these programs will continue to enroll very large numbers of minority students. One reminder that I take away from this experience is that just getting mad is rarely, if ever, an effective response to a challenge—in this instance, a challenge to end racial exclusivity. Rather, we need to respond by reaffirming the basic objectives we are seeking to serve and by finding the most effective ways of achieving them. We definitely need to "stay the course," but not by being foolishly confrontational.

Third, we need to resist assaults on race-sensitive programs that are based on inadequately documented critiques of existing policies. We should reaffirm

---

8. See Robert Becker, "Black Enrollment at U of Illinois Rebounding from Last Year," *Chicago Tribune* (June 7, 2005): C3.

the results of soundly based research and not be too quick to allow others to call into question well-established findings by reference to new work that has yet to be properly vetted. I refer to the renewed discussion in the law school context of the so-called "mismatch" hypothesis, which argues against affirmative action on the ground that it entices minority students into programs that are too demanding for them, with bad results (low graduation rates) for the minority students in question. Others are in the process of challenging the methodology of Sander's law school study, and I have nothing specific to contribute to that debate.[9] But I can report that my colleague, Nirupama Rao, has just completed an analysis of recently compiled data for the 1995 entering cohorts of undergraduates at 29 academically selective colleges and universities in the expanded College & Beyond database, and her findings reaffirm the flat rejection of the mismatch hypothesis reported in *The Shape of the River*.[10] There is no evidence to support the mismatch conjecture. Indeed, the general implication of the earlier analysis and of these new results is that, in choosing among undergraduate institutions, minority students are well advised to attend the most selective institution that will admit them.[11]

---

9. Richard Sander, "A Systematic Analysis of Affirmative Action in American Law Schools," *Stanford Law Review*, 57 (November 2004): 367–483. A collection of responses to Sander's article, by authors including David B. Wilkins, William C. Kidder, David L. Chambers, Richard O. Lempert, Timothy T. Clydesdale, Ian Ayres, and Richard Brooks, can be found in the May 2005 issue of the *Stanford Law Review*. Economists Jesse Rothstein at Princeton and Albert Yoon at Yale, who contend that Sander's conclusions are unsupported by his analyses, are embarking on a study that will use the same data—principally the Bar Passage Study (BPS), based on LSAC's survey of students who entered law school in 1994, plus data about the respondents who passed the bar exam, to analyze with greater empirical rigor the effect of attending a selective law school on black students' academic outcomes.

10. William G. Bowen and Derek Bok, *The Shape of the River: Long-Term Consequences of Considering Race in College and University Admissions* (Princeton, N.J.: Princeton University Press, 1998), 59–68.

11. Using raw, unadjusted data, Rao finds that graduation rates for both black and Hispanic students with SATs in specified ranges increase with school selectivity overall, but that the pattern is not entirely consistent. However, once controls are added for gender, socioeconomic status, and characteristics of individual schools, the results become entirely consistent. Otherwise, comparable black students in every SAT range graduate at higher rates the more selective the school that they attend. When she studies rank-in-class, Rao finds that, as one would expect, both white and black students pay a "rank-in-class" penalty for attending more selective schools where they have to compete with large numbers of exceptionally well-qualified classmates. Interestingly, black students pay a somewhat higher price than otherwise comparable white students in moving from Sel-3 to Sel-2 schools, but they pay a smaller price than the white students in moving from Sel-2 schools to the (most selective) Sel-1 schools. (For additional information on this new research, contact Nirupama Rao, at the Andrew W. Mellon Foundation.) We should also recall that survey data reported in *The Shape of the River* demonstrated that even if minority students earn, on average, lower grades than their high-achieving classmates at selective schools, they earn advanced degrees at high rates and go on to do well in later life in terms of earnings, life satisfaction, and civic participation.

Nevertheless, there is a real issue here, even though it has nothing to do with the mismatch hypothesis. In his study of law school results, Sander is right to call attention to the disappointing academic performance of minority students. Indeed, our recent work shows that, in general, minority students in undergraduate programs continue to underperform academically (by which we mean that academic outcomes for minority students lag academic outcomes for other students with similar observed characteristics). Underperformance appears to have declined somewhat between the 1989 and 1995 entering cohorts, but it still exists—at all kinds of schools and in all SAT ranges.[12] Thus, as a fourth "to do," I conclude that we should focus on the roots of this troubling problem of underperformance and find ways of attacking it—of the kinds pioneered by Freeman Hrabowski at the University of Maryland and by our colleagues in South Africa.[13] Some of the lessons to be learned by studying the academic experiences of students from modest socioeconomic backgrounds may also turn out to be highly relevant to our interest in improving the academic outcomes of minority students.

Socioeconomic Status

My most recent research has focused on socioeconomic status, college enrollment, and educational attainment. It should be no surprise to anyone that in today's world, America's premier colleges and universities, including the great public universities, serve mainly the children of the privileged classes. At the

12. Some people confuse the mismatch hypothesis with underperformance. They are two entirely different concepts. The mismatch hypothesis could be one explanation for underperformance by minority students if these students underperformed at schools where average SAT scores were appreciably higher than their own scores, but did not underperform at schools where school SAT scores and their SAT scores "matched." But this is not what the evidence shows. As we point out in the text, underperformance exists *at every SAT range within every selectivity range*. It is an endemic phenomenon that does not correlate with the relation between an individual's SAT score and the average SAT at the school the student attends; underperformance cannot be explained by claiming that minority students are attending schools where they are overchallenged.

13. Ian Scott, Nan Yeld, Janice McMillan, and Martin Hall, "Equality and Excellence in Higher Education: The Case of the University of Cape Town," pp. 261–284 in Bowen, Kurzweil, and Tobin, *Equity and Excellence in American Higher Education*; Freeman Hrabowski, "Supporting the Talented Tenth: The Role of Research Universities in Promoting Higher Achievement Among Minorities in Science and Engineering," David Dodds Henry Lecture, University of Illinois at Urbana-Champaign, November 5, 2003; Freeman Hrabowski, Kenneth I. Maton, and Geoffrey L. Greif, *Beating the Odds: Raising Academically Successful African American Males* (New York: Oxford University Press, 1998); Freeman Hrabowski, Kenneth I. Maton, Monica L. Greene, and Geoffrey L. Greif, *Overcoming the Odds: Raising Academically Successful African American Young Women* (New York: Oxford University Press, 2002).

19 selective colleges and universities we studied, only about 10 percent of the students come from low-income families and an even smaller fraction are first-generation college-goers. Very high fractions come from well-educated families with substantial incomes.

In considering what to do about this discomforting reality, my first suggestion is that we work harder to explain convincingly why such disproportionate access to educational opportunity is a serious problem for the country. There is, to be sure, an issue of fundamental fairness to be confronted, and there is a corresponding need for social mobility in a democratic society. This is, as it were, the moral/social/political rationale for extending opportunity more broadly. But there is also a more mundane, economic rationale. Increasingly economies, and certainly the U.S. economy, are driven by what Sir Arthur Lewis called "reliance on brain" (or, if you prefer, trained intelligence). Yet the United States can no longer simply assume that its educational system, and its educated workforce, will be preeminent. Incremental educational attainment in the United States (measured, for instance, by the percentage of the U.S. population 25- to 29-year-olds who have completed college) is no longer increasing at a steady rate, as it did for so many decades. At the same time that educational attainment is plateauing in the United States, it is continuing to rise rapidly in many other parts of the world. The United States is no longer at the top of the world tables in educational attainment of those 25 to 34 years of age, and it is far below a number of other countries in the ratio of first university natural science and engineering degrees to the 24-year-old population.[14]

What is happening? There is ample evidence, we believe, that America today confronts a major supply-side block in college preparedness that limits our country's ability to increase educational attainment. How else are we to explain the plateauing of educational attainment in the United States at the same time that the returns to college education are so high? Put another way, the question is: Why do we observe a pronounced lack of market response to such a compelling economic opportunity? The ability to pay for education, and the existence of credit constraints, are, as economists always note, surely part of the explanation, but no one seems to think that they are anything like the whole story—or

---

14. In 2002, the percentage of the 25- to 34-year-old population in the United States that had attained tertiary education was 39, close to that of South Korea, New Zealand, Norway, Finland, Sweden, and Belgium. With attainment at or just above 50 percent, Canada and Japan were at the top of the list (OECD, *Education at a Glance 2004*). In the United States, the ratio of first university degrees in the natural sciences and engineering to the 24-year-old population is 5.7. The ratio exceeds 10 in a number of countries in Europe and Asia (Appendix Table 2-33, *Science and Engineering Indicators 2004* [Arlington, Va.: National Science Foundation], http://www.nsf.gov/sbe/srs/seind04/start.htm).

even the main part of the story. More consequential factors include college preparedness in all of its dimensions (health, attitudes at home, motivation, the availability of information, the quality of elementary and secondary education, out-of-school enrichment opportunities, and residential and social segregation). College preparedness varies dramatically with socioeconomic status, as we have documented in our recent book. Students from the bottom-income quartile are only *one-sixth* as likely as students from the top-income quartile to be in what we define as the credible pool of candidates for admission to academically selective colleges and universities; students who lack a parent with some experience of college are *one-seventh* as likely as other students to be in the credible pool.

The connections, on the one hand, between socioeconomic status and educational attainment and, on the other hand, between educational attainment and economic competitiveness, are crystal clear; and there is a crucially important political reason for emphasizing this nexus. One of my most knowledgeable friends, at a discussion of the findings in *Equity and Excellence*, expressed pessimism at the prospect of mobilizing society to address disparities in opportunity because, he said, only a small fraction of people in the United States today really care about "liberal" goals such as fairness and social mobility; he believes that most (he suggested 80 percent) care mainly about how they themselves are doing. That may or may not be correct, but in any case it is surely a political mistake to base the case for addressing inequalities in access to a high-quality education on moral or social considerations alone. Why be so single-minded? The most conservative, market-oriented American should see that unless the United States does better in educating more students from low-income, out-of-the-mainstream families to a high standard, we will lose out, over time, to other countries in the worldwide competition for talent. That brute fact alone should make it clear *across the political spectrum* why we cannot afford to accept supply-side blocks on educational attainment. Looking ahead, demographic trends only reinforce what I have been saying. Reliance on children of well-educated, high-income (mostly white) families to fill the educational pipeline will not suffice. Check out the numbers.

Let me now assume that we succeed in marshaling at least some number of troops, conservatives and liberals alike, who will support efforts to augment opportunity for students from modest backgrounds. What programs and policies will do the job?

At the most fundamental level the only way, in the long run, to solve the college preparation gap is to attack it directly—through improvements in the schools that disadvantaged young people attend, in the neighborhoods in which they live, and in the health care and other services on which they, like everyone else, depend. In terms of schooling, recent results achieved by fifth graders in some of New York's poorest districts offer some grounds for hope. Both math and reading scores have improved dramatically, and it appears to have been good organization, and a lot of hard work, that did the job—no magic wands were in evidence.[15] The Gates Foundation is mounting a major, highly ambitious effort to see if investing in smaller schools will make a large, measurable difference in high school completion and college preparedness. And there are other initiatives in many states and communities. But these "bedrock" programs, essential as they are, will require years to affect college enrollments, and we do not want to lose more generations of promising candidates from modest circumstances in the interim.

Governmental programs and policies, at the federal, the state, and even the municipal levels, clearly have a major role to play "in the here and now," and we catalog a number of opportunities to do better in these realms in our *Equity and Excellence* book. But my own knowledge of these programs is very much secondhand, and I would not serve you well by simply repeating propositions regarding incentives and cost-effectiveness that many in the audience can assess much more knowledgeably than I can. (I cannot resist, however, saying that I think *completion*, not just starting out, matters enormously, and that policymakers need to focus more on attainment, and on reducing attrition, not just on first-year enrollments.) Please do not, in any case, misinterpret my failure to discuss governmental initiatives as implying that they are anything less than tremendously important. My focus will be on educational institutions, and especially on the academically selective colleges and universities that I know fairly well (public and private), even as we all understand that if Harvard's enrollment profile were to "look like America" tomorrow, the needle that tracks national numbers would move hardly at all. There would be consequences, nonetheless, that transcend aggregate numbers. The leading colleges and universities continue to be important pathways to opportunities of every kind and, as admired institutions, to play leadership roles within American higher education. They send strong messages (for better or for worse), and such "signaling" effects should not be underestimated.

Looking at the question of "what is to be done" from the perspective of the gatekeeping function of leading selective institutions,[16] there are three levers that can be used.

---

15. See David M. Herszenhorn and Susan Saulny, "What Lifted Fifth-Grade Scores? Schools Say Lots of Hard Work," *New York Times* (June 12, 2005): A1.

16. In focusing on how the gatekeeping function is to be managed, I set aside the question of what these institutions can do to improve precollegiate preparation through programs of every kind, ranging from the activities of schools of education in preparing teachers to tutoring and mentoring services provided by faculty and students.

First is the admissions process itself, and the criteria used to "craft a class." In *Equity and Excellence*, we point to a surprising disjunction between the rhetoric used to describe institutional commitments to diversity of all kinds and present-day realities. The rhetoric regularly includes language like "admissions officials give special attention to...applicants from economically and/or culturally disadvantaged backgrounds...and those who would be the first in their families to attend any college..."[17] What is striking is the juxtaposition of this clear statement of intent with the equally clear empirical finding that, for the 1995 entering cohort at the selective schools in our study, there is absolutely no admissions advantage associated with coming from a poor family and only a very small advantage (about 4 percentage points) associated with being a first-generation college-goer. These estimates are all based on an "other things equal" analysis. It is instructive to compare the corresponding admissions advantages enjoyed by the typical recruited athlete (about 31 percentage points), a member of an underrepresented minority group (27 points), and a legacy (19 points).[18]

We do not believe that admissions officials are dissembling when they suggest (or even insist) that their results are different from the empirical findings that we have assembled. In most cases, admissions offices lack the data needed to rigorously compare the characteristics of those offered admission and the characteristics of all those in the applicant pool (an important observation, we think, in its own right). Moreover, there is a natural human tendency to live in "the anecdote range"; these schools do enroll many wonderful students from poor families and we like to talk about them. The empirical findings are also affected significantly, we think, by the presence in the admissions process of "champions" for the other special groups who enjoy sizable admissions advantages—and the lack of similarly visible champions for applicants from modest backgrounds. Finally, it is entirely possible—likely, in fact—that applicants at given SAT levels from well-to-do families will present more impressive nonacademic credentials than applicants from poor families, who are less likely to have had opportunities to be outstanding musicians, leaders of clubs that have traveled the world, social activists, and so on. These other qualifications surely deserve some weight, but we wonder how fully people recognize the effects on the socioeconomic profile of the class of taking these wealth-related qualifications into account.

---

17. Quotation is from the amicus brief submitted to the U.S. Supreme Court in *Grutter v. Bollinger* et al. and *Gratz v. Bollinger* et al. by Harvard University, Brown University, the University of Chicago, Dartmouth College, Duke University, the University of Pennsylvania, Princeton University, and Yale University.

18. These numbers are based on new logit probabilities calculated by Nirupama Rao; they differ vary slightly from those in *Equity and Excellence*, 166.

In any event, one (purely hypothetical) approach to doing more in the admissions process for students from modest backgrounds would be to put what we have called a "thumb" on the scale when considering their applications. By this we mean simply using individualized assessments in the case of these poor students analogous to the assessments used, for example, in considering legacy applicants; the goal would be to seek a rough equivalence between poor students and legacies in the odds of being admitted at any given SAT level. Heuristically, there is, it seems to us, a nice symbolism between giving the same "break" to those who have overcome so many obstacles that schools give to the most privileged applicants with the same observable credentials. This approach would give the biggest admissions break to those from modest backgrounds who have really excelled, since this is the approach used in considering legacy applicants. Simulations suggest that this approach would raise the percentage of students from low-income families from about 10 percent of the class to about 18 percent. Any number of other algorithms could of course be employed, and schools should use whatever size or shape of thumb that makes sense to them. All that we are suggesting is that high-achieving students from modest backgrounds deserve at least some break when being considered for admissions—it would be splendid if rhetoric and reality were brought into closer balance.

Before moving on, I want to mention an important political point made by Amy Gutmann at a discussion of this topic held at Brookings in April. Amy said (and I paraphrase): "Let's not focus solely on the bottom-income quartile. Students from the second and third quartiles are also underrepresented, and we should avoid 'dissing' the middle class." Amy is right about the underrepresentation of the broad middle class, and her political sensitivity is also right on point. We are certainly not opposed to making greater efforts to admit more applicants from these middle-income groups. But everyone needs to recognize that it is students from the bottom quartile who have leapt over the highest hurdles in getting into the credible pool of applicants and that, for example, applicants from the third quartile are 2.5 times more likely to get into our "credible" pool than are those from the bottom quartile; those from the second quartile are also more likely to be in the pool, but their advantage over the bottom quartile is much less pronounced. Perhaps the best place to draw some kind of line is between the bottom and top halves of the income distribution.

The second lever is the provision of generous financial aid, and I presume that all of you are aware that some of the wealthier private schools (such as Princeton, Harvard, and Yale) and some of the more aggressive public universities (such as the University of Virginia) have replaced loans with full grant aid for students below some income threshold. We applaud this initiative, if the funds are available to sustain it, but we wonder if this is the most cost-effective use of available resources. The admissions yields for low-income admittees are already high, and we do not know how much difference, on the margin, the more generous aid packages really make. One heretical idea would be to redeploy some of the grant aid in the, by now, very generous basic grant packages (expecting some parental contribution and/or some use of loans) in order to free up funds that could be used to cover the additional financial aid costs associated with enrolling the modestly increased number of applicants with need who might be admitted by means of the "thumb" approach.

The third lever is a more aggressive effort to provide information that would, for example, help students and their families get over "sticker shock" and appreciate the extent to which need-based financial aid is available. Additional investments in recruitment, designed to enlarge applicant pools, are highly desirable, and we have nothing but praise for them. What remains to be learned is which approaches are most effective, and whether additional investments should be made in multi-institutional recruitment/enrichment efforts of the kind being tried out by Gary Simons and his Leadership Enterprise for a Diverse America (LEDA) program.

More generally, we are strongly in favor of monitoring and assessing the growing range of initiatives of this kind. It is important to acquire a sharper understanding than I think anyone has today of what really works and what doesn't work in different settings. As much as the "missionary" individual recruitment effort is to be applauded, what we need are systematic strategies that are not dependent on the charisma of particular individuals. Public policy research must identify interventions that are replicable. It is not enough to assume that good intentions will necessarily produce good results—or, put more accurately, will produce results good enough to justify the particular investment as compared with other possible investments of scarce resources.

Having suggested several approaches worth considering, individually and in concert with one another, I want now to voice a few cautions.

- We should be very careful not to overvalue numerical goals such as raising the percentage of students in the class who come from the bottom income quartile to some arbitrarily set threshold. This caution mirrors the warning that Sarah Turner and others have voiced about overweighting the value of Pell Grant data in assessing how particular schools are doing in extending opportunity.[19]

---

19. Jeffrey Tebbs and Sarah Turner, "College Education for Low-Income Students: A Caution on the Use of Data on Pell Grant Recipients," University of Virginia, preliminary draft (September 10, 2004).

So much depends on the location of a particular school, on the demographics of the surrounding region, and on institutional history. Pushing too hard to reach a numerical goal can also lead to admissions decisions that put the likely success of a student too much at risk.

- A related concern is that in seeking to reach pre-set goals, or just in trying to do everything one can to increase socioeconomic diversity, schools may not think hard enough about their real objectives. At the risk of being misunderstood, and annoying large numbers of friends, let me ask, for example, if we really believe that a state university should view as equivalent enrolling Student A, who is an out-of-state applicant from an immigrant family that is poor but advantaged culturally, and Student B, who is from a family in a poor rural region of the state that has been poor for decades and has no experience of higher education. Sympathetic as I am to both of these students, I am even more taken by the case of Student B, since I think that some emphasis should be placed on achieving real intergenerational mobility. To generalize further, I am increasingly skeptical that family income per se is the right measure of disadvantage. We can all think of cases of individuals from families that do not earn a great deal of money, but that have had other advantages (the children of missionaries may be the classic example). We certainly want to enroll such students, but we will need to work even harder to enroll students from culturally deprived backgrounds that have somehow made it into the credible applicant pool—through the efforts of a special teacher, the determination of a mother who would insist that for her children there would be "no limits," or sheer grit.

- The last caution I want to mention has to do with issues of social discomfort and isolation. In thinking about obstacles to the enrollment of more students from nonmainline backgrounds, we need to take into account not just academic considerations (and fears), and not just worries about being able to pay bills and stay out of debt, but also concerns about the prospect of social isolation—of feeling entirely out-of-place and uncomfortable on a campus where BMWs are much in evidence and socially exclusive social systems affect campus life. These considerations tend to be more serious barriers at schools in bucolic settings than in urban institutions, but they are real and cannot be dismissed. In many discussions of our book, we were reminded over and over again of how acutely students from modest backgrounds feel about these kinds of social issues. And how often, in the past, discomfort led to attrition or disappointing performance.

Let me now put some "clothes" on these rather abstract observations by quoting from a letter I received a few weeks ago from a faculty member at Bryn Mawr who had read part of our book and wanted us to know of her personal odyssey. She is a professor of mathematics, and she thought (rightly) that her own experiences might highlight some of the continuing challenges that we face in promoting opportunity. Here is part of what she wrote:

> My [Chicago] high school was populated primarily by the children of Polish, Lithuanian, Swedish, Greek, and German immigrants, most of whom held blue-collar jobs. Gage Park was the last all-white high school in the city. I was one of about three or four Jewish students in the school, a minority among minorities. Although I was ranked first in my class for four years, I do not recall receiving any encouragement to attend college. In fact, I was in a secretarial track until I realized that I could not take shorthand, and that my grades would suffer accordingly. I asked a counselor to allow me to switch into a physics course, in order to protect my grades; the change inadvertently placed me in the college-preparatory track.
>
> In our senior year, a few of my girlfriends announced that they were applying to the University of Illinois at Urbana-Champaign, and I followed suit. Most of the girls in my class would either become secretaries (an avenue closed to me for obvious reasons), or go to other state schools to study elementary education. Only a few of the boys I knew went to college; those who did not were drafted and went to Vietnam. My friends and I started college in February, thoroughly naïve about the profound culture shock that awaited us. I can only imagine what would have happened to us at an Ivy League institution, or an elite liberal arts college.
>
> At Urbana, we encountered relatively sophisticated suburban kids who, compared to us, had a great deal of money and privilege. I was terrified that I would not do well academically, since I had no idea how my education had prepared me for college. The academic challenges proved far easier to navigate than the social ones. Despite my 4.0 GPA, I dropped out by the middle of my second year. Another Gage Park student, a brilliant scientist and artist who had finished second in the Illinois State Science Fair, left before the end of the first year. After working for six months, I applied to the University of Illinois at Chicago, where I completed my bachelor's degree. The diversity and anonymity of a commuter campus suited me well. Thanks to the encouragement of a particular professor

I encountered in my junior year, I stayed at UIC and went on to earn M.S. and Ph.D. degrees in mathematics. Although my parents ultimately were very proud of my achievements, at the time they were frustrated by my insistence on becoming what they viewed as a "professional student," and were relieved to see that eventually I could earn a living doing what I loved.

Through a University of Illinois connection, I landed a tenure-track job at Tufts University, where I remained for five years before moving to Bryn Mawr...From the moment I began teaching, I was struck by a sense of injustice and unfairness on behalf of my fellow Gage Park students. Before, I had no metric by which to gauge how bright they really were. However, teaching well-prepared students, I realized that many of my friends would have excelled academically at the elite institutions where I now taught.

"Finally" (the most beautiful word in the English language), I want to end by repeating an injunction that I take very seriously. In making the case for enrolling—and graduating—more students from families of modest background, there is also one thing (among many, no doubt) that we should *not* do: namely, suggest that paying more attention to socioeconomic status will eliminate the need for race-based affirmative action any time soon. Recognition of the most obvious demographic proposition—that minority families are heavily concentrated at the bottom of the income distribution—has led some to suggest that the way to get past the need for race-sensitive admissions is to give more preference to applicants from poor families, white or minority. Again, we should check out the numbers. Simulations for the 19 schools in our study demonstrate that giving low-income students the same admissions preference that is given today to legacies would increase the percentage of enrolled students from underrepresented racial minorities above what it would be in the absence of *any* racial or socioeconomic preferences by only about two percentage points; the overall result would be to cut minority enrollment at the undergraduate level to about *half* what it is today. At graduate and professional levels, the impact would probably be even greater.

In short, paying attention to class and background, which we strongly favor, is, at this juncture in our history, no substitute for paying attention to race. As I have said before, Americans always seek the painless alternative, and it is much easier for most people to be sympathetic to economic disadvantage than it is for them to understand and address the more deeply rooted and emotionally challenging issues that are due in such large part to what Glenn Loury has called the "unlovely history" of race in America. But surely it ought to be possible to think about opportunity from more than a single perspective—to recognize that the river of opportunity has tributaries of many hues and many kinds. There is also the matter of attitude. It is clearly necessary to focus on the difficulties and the challenges involved in helping this river wind to the sea, however measured its progress. But we should also be grateful for the privilege of addressing such fundamental questions, and we should be permitted to take some satisfaction from trying to do the right things for the right reasons.

Was Justice O'Connor Right?
Race and Highly Selective College Admissions in 25 Years[1]

Alan B. Krueger, Jesse Rothstein, and Sarah Turner

In her opinion in *Grutter v. Bollinger*, Justice Sandra Day O'Connor concluded that affirmative action in college admissions is justifiable, but not in perpetuity: "We expect that 25 years from now, the use of racial preferences will no longer be necessary to further the interest [in student body diversity] approved today."

The rate at which racial gaps in precollegiate academic achievement can plausibly be expected to erode is a matter of considerable uncertainty. In this essay, we attempt to evaluate the plausibility of Justice O'Connor's conjecture by projecting the racial composition of the 2025 elite college applicant pool. Our projections extrapolate past trends on two important margins: Gaps between the economic resources of black and white students' families, and narrowing of test score gaps between black and white students with similar family incomes. Just as the last decades have seen considerable narrowing of gaps on each margin, further progress can be expected over the next quarter century.

Our central question is whether this progress will plausibly be fast enough to validate Justice O'Connor's prediction. We are well aware of the hazards inherent in our exercise: No such distant projections can be definitive. Nevertheless, by relying on reasonable historical assumptions that are arguably optimistic, we develop a baseline case for assessing the likelihood of O'Connor's forecast.

We conclude that under reasonable assumptions, African American students will continue to be substantially underrepresented among the most qualified college applicants for the foreseeable future. The magnitude of the underrepresentation is likely to shrink—in our most optimistic simulation, somewhat over half of the gap that would be opened by the elimination of race preferences will be closed by the projected improvement in black achievement.

---

1. This essay is based on Krueger, Rothstein, and Turner ("Race, Income, and College in 25 Years: Evaluating Justice O'Connor's Conjecture," *American Law and Economics Review* [forthcoming]), which contains methodological details and additional analyses not included here. We thank Bill Bowen for suggesting this topic; Martin Kurzweil and Nirupama S. Rao for help with the Mellon Expanded College and Beyond data; and the UCLA Center on Education Policy and Evaluation, the Russell Sage Foundation, the Carnegie Corporation, and the Princeton Industrial Relations Section for generous research support. We are grateful to Orley Ashenfelter, Humphrey Doermann, Martin Kurzweil, Gary Solon, and Jacob Vigdor for excellent comments.

Still, it seems unlikely that today's level of racial diversity will be achievable without some form of continuing affirmative action. If the Supreme Court follows through with O'Connor's stated intention to ban affirmative action in 25 years, and if colleges do not adjust in other ways (such as reducing the importance of numerical qualifications to admissions), we project substantial declines in the representation of African Americans among admitted students at selective institutions.

Our analysis proceeds from the assumption that the most likely future course will resemble past trends. Substantial changes in educational policy, in school effectiveness, and in income inequality would all have important effects on black test score distributions and on the admissions landscape.[2]

Recent Trends in Racial Inequality

Currently, racial gaps in precollegiate achievement are extremely large, and very few black students would be admitted to elite colleges under race-blind admissions rules. Figure 1a shows the distribution of SAT scores among black and white students in

Figure 1a. SAT distributions among black and white test-takers, 2000

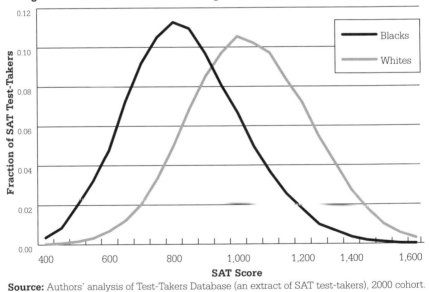

Source: Authors' analysis of Test-Takers Database (an extract of SAT test-takers), 2000 cohort.

2. There are several additional limitations to our study. First, we restrict our attention to black and white students. In light of the United States' distinct historical legacy of racial policies, the representation of African Americans in elite colleges is of unique interest; in any event, projections are hazardous for groups experiencing substantial continuing immigration. Second, we focus on selective institutions. Thus, we say little about aggregate college attainment trends, which primarily reflect outcomes at nonselective, open-access institutions. Third, we neglect aspects of the college pipeline other than the admissions decision itself. Though application and matriculation behavior will certainly change—perhaps even in response to the trends that we study—these are not our focus.

2000. The black–white gap in mean scores is approximately 201 points, or almost exactly one standard deviation. More relevant is the top of the distribution, as the selective schools that are our focus admit few students with scores below 1200. As shown in Figure 1b, only 4 percent of students who earn SAT scores of 1200 are black (as compared with 14.3 percent of all SAT test-takers), and the fraction is even lower for higher scores; only 2.4 percent of students with scores exceeding 1200 are black.[3]

Historically comparable data on SAT score distributions are not readily available, but Figure 2 shows black–white test score gaps on the National

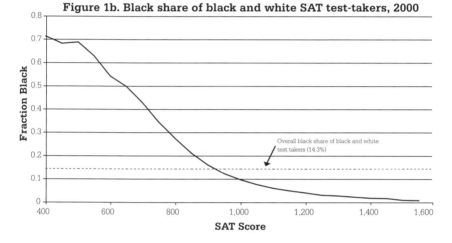

Figure 1b. Black share of black and white SAT test-takers, 2000

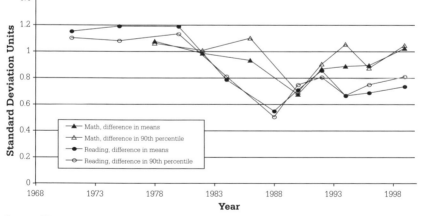

Figure 2. Trends in black–white gaps in student achievement at age 17, in standard deviation units

Source: National Assessment of Educational Progress results (National Center for Education Statistics, 1999).

3. Here and elsewhere, the fraction refers to the black share of black and white students; students of other races are omitted from all computations.

Assessment of Education Progress (NAEP) assessment since 1970. In that year, the average 17-year-old black student scored over 1.1 standard deviations below the average white student in reading. For reasons that are not well understood, this gap was stable in the 1970s, shrunk dramatically in the 1980s, and has grown somewhat since around 1990. Today, the black–white gap stands at about three quarters of a standard deviation in reading, and is even higher in math.

An obvious partial explanation for the persistence of the test score gap is the continuing gap in economic resources between black and white students' families. Black workers earn substantially less, on average, than do whites, though the differential has slowly narrowed. The earnings gap between black and white men was 38 percent in 1960 and 26 percent in 2000. This progress has been largely offset, however, by deterioration in black family structures, as single parenthood has risen and the number of children in two-earner families has consequently fallen. The gap in total family income between black and white children has hardly moved in three decades.

Affirmative Action and College Access for Black Students

The precise mechanics of selective college admissions are closely guarded secrets.[4] Still, by examining average admissions probabilities among groups defined by important determinants, like SAT scores, it is possible to get an idea of the current roles of race and academic qualifications in admissions. We focus on four groups of colleges and universities: most selective, highly selective, and moderately selective private institutions, and elite public universities.[5] It must be emphasized that these labels are relative characterizations; even the least selective group in our typology is extremely selective by any national standard.

Admissions profiles are shown in Figure 3. These show evidence of substantial affirmative action preferences, with black admissions rates exceeding those of white students with much higher SAT scores. Table 1 shows the current black share of admitted students in each group and our estimate of what it would be if black students were admitted according to the profiles seen for white applicants.

---

4. Jerome Karabel, *The Chosen: The Hidden History of Admission and Exclusion at Harvard, Yale, and Princeton* (Boston: Houghton Mifflin, 2005).

5. William Bowen, Martin Kurzweil, and Eugene Tobin have generously provided us extracts from the Expanded College and Beyond (ECB) study of the 1995 admissions cycle that was assembled by the Andrew W. Mellon Foundation and used in their book, *Equity and Excellence in Higher Education* (Charlottesville, Va.: University of Virginia Press, 2005). The most selective private institutions are Harvard, Princeton, and Yale; the highly selective are Columbia, the University of Pennsylvania, Swarthmore, and Williams; and the moderately selective are Barnard, Bowdoin, Middlebury, Oberlin, Pomona, and Wellesley. Public universities are Pennsylvania State University and the University of Virginia. Confidentiality requirements prevent a more disaggregated presentation.

Figure 3. Admission rates by type of institution, SAT score, and race

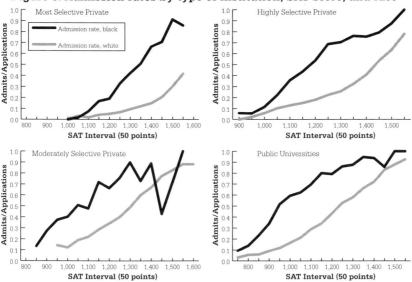

Source: Authors' calculations from the Expanded College and Beyond database.

Table 1. Black share of admitted students at elite institutions, 2000, actual and with race-blind admission rules

	Most Selective Colleges	Highly Selective Colleges	Moderately Selective Colleges	Public Universities
Actual	0.171	0.142	0.094	0.118
With race-blind admissions	0.051	0.060	0.051	0.053
Change with shift to race-blind admissions	-70 %	-58 %	-46 %	-55 %

Notes: "Most selective" is a composite of Harvard, Princeton, and Yale; "highly selective" is a composite of Columbia, the University of Pennsylvania, Swarthmore, and Williams; "moderately selective" is a composite of Barnard, Bowdoin, Middlebury, Oberlin, Pomona, and Wellesley; and "public" is a composite of the University of Virginia and Pennsylvania State.

With race-blind admissions, black representation at the four clusters of schools would fall by 70, 58, 46, and 55 percent, respectively.

Projections
Test Scores

Our projections of likely future improvement in the black relative test score distribution proceed in two stages. First, we estimate the degree to which black family income gains can be expected to close the test score gap shown in Figure 1. As SAT scores depend heavily on family income, predictable increases in black families' relative incomes will lead to increases in black students' relative scores. Second, we incorporate plausible reductions in the black–white gap in test scores among children with the same family incomes by extrapolating the trend in NAEP scores shown in Figure 2.[6] Reasonable people may differ in their projections of the likely rate of future convergence on either margin; our estimates are meant to indicate what sort of progress will be required to obtain desired admissions results.

Among families with children ages 15 to 17 in the 2000 census, black families had incomes 54 percent less than white families, on average. Estimates of the intergenerational transmission of incomes indicate that, on average, somewhere between 40 and 60 percent of the gap between a family's income and the mean income will be closed with each generation.[7] We take the center of this range, which implies that the black–white income gap will decline by half with each successive generation. This does a good job of fitting the black–white gap in male earnings in recent decades, which fell from 37 percent in 1969 to 19 percent in 1999.[8] As noted above, however, it overstates recent progress in family incomes, and our assumption that the gap on this margin will fall by half in the next quarter century is thus probably optimistic.

Halving the black–white gap in log family incomes will have disproportionate effects on the number of black families at the very high income levels from which elite college applicants are largely drawn. We estimate, for example, that the fraction of black families with incomes between $80,000 and $100,000 will increase by 69 percent (from 4.7 percent to 8.0 percent). Because children from families with higher incomes are more likely to take the SAT and more likely to earn high scores, increases in black family incomes will yield increases in the number of high-scoring black students. To quantify this, we assume that the "new" high-income black students will have test-taking rates and score distributions like those of current high-income black students. When we apply the projected

---

6. "Results Over Time—NAEP 1999 Long-Term Trend Summary Data Tables," National Center for Education Statistics (1999), http://nces.ed.gov/nationsreportcard/tables/Ltt1999/. For details of our methods and descriptions of the underlying data, interested readers are referred to Alan B. Krueger, Jesse Rothstein, and Sarah Turner, "Race, Income, and College in 25 Years: Evaluating Justice O'Connor's Conjecture," *American Law and Economics Review* (forthcoming).

7. As is conventional, we work with the logarithm of family income rather than the level; all figures in this paragraph refer to log incomes. Bhashkar Mazumder, "Earnings Mobility in the U.S.: A New Look at Intergenerational Mobility," mimeo (2000); Gary Solon, "Intergenerational Mobility in the Labor Market," in *Handbook of Labor Economics*, Vol. 3A (Orley Ashenfelter and David Card, eds), (1999): 1761–1800, Elsevier Science: Amsterdam; Laura Chadwick and Gary Solon, "Intergenerational Income Mobility Among Daughters," *American Economic Review* 92, No. 1. (March 2002): 335–344; Gary Solon, "Cross-Country Differences in Intergenerational Earnings Mobility," *Journal of Economic Perspectives* 16, No. 3 (Summer 2002): 59–66.

8. Alan B. Krueger, "The Supreme Court Finds the 'Mushball Middle' on Affirmative Action," *New York Times* (July 23, 2003): C2.

future income distribution, we compute that black average scores will be about 19 points higher than they are today, and that the black SAT participation rate will rise by 0.7 percent. Figure 4a shows the current black SAT score distribution and the projected future distribution (labeled "income growth only"), while Figure 4b shows the impact on the fraction black at each SAT score.[9]

Figure 4a. Projections of future black SAT score distribution

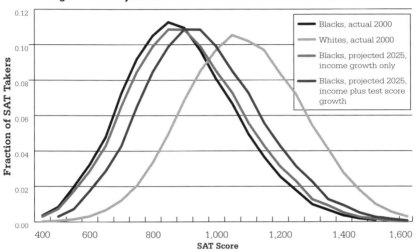

Figure 4b. Projections of black share of SAT test-takers, by score

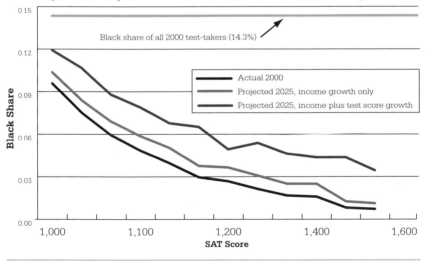

9. One disconnect between our simulation and the educational process is worth noting. Although the reasons why family income affects student performance on the SAT are unclear, it is quite likely that the entire stream of family income over a child's time at home is relevant, not just income in the year he or she takes the SAT. Unfortunately, we lack data on family income in earlier years. Many of the intergenerational convergence estimates in the literature apply to long run, not annual, income.

The way to interpret our projection is that we increase black families' incomes by the amount predicted from the narrowing of the black–white gap over a generation, while holding everything else—the distribution of white incomes and the distribution of test scores conditional on income and race—constant. Of course, real income growth will raise both black and white incomes over the next quarter century, and black and white mean test scores may evolve in tandem. Absent changes in inequality, however, this will not affect the shape of the distribution. Our approach indexes black income and test score growth against that of whites, and we implicitly assume that admissions standards adjust to maintain each institution's selectivity.

Income is not the only source of potential changes in admissions qualifications, so the "income growth only" estimate in Figures 4a and 4b might be seen as a lower bound. An alternative includes some closing of the black–white test score gap within income groups. To make our projections, we assume that conditional-on-income test score gaps will close as much in the next 25 years as the unconditional gaps did over the last 25 years. The black–white gap in NAEP scores has shrunk by an average of about 1 percent of a standard deviation per year (with faster progress in reading and slower progress in math). If this average rate of progress continues for 25 years, we should see the racial gap in SAT scores fall by 50 points.

The final series in Figures 4a and 4b shows the combined impact of this and income convergence. This almost certainly overestimates the extent of black score growth over the next quarter century. As Figure 2 indicates, essentially all of the progress over the last 25 years in NAEP scores occurred in the 1980s, and the gap grew during the 1990s. It requires substantial optimism to believe that future progress will occur at the rate seen over the full NAEP period rather than the much slower rate seen recently, particularly as we are assuming that this progress will be in addition to that generated by income convergence.

Admissions Projections

Our interest is in how the projected changes in the relative distribution of the academic achievement (measured by test scores) of black and white students will alter the relative representation of black and white students among those likely to be admitted to selective colleges and universities under race-blind admission policies. Our income convergence estimate implies a 33 percent increase in the number of black students who score above 1200 (over today's low level); when we additionally apply NAEP trends, we project a 109 percent increase. Even under this counterfactual, however, the proportion of blacks scoring above 1200 will be about one-third of the corresponding proportion of whites, with more extreme underrepresentation at higher scores.

The next step is to convert the projected change in the SAT distribution to admissions rates. We model expected admissions to "composite" schools corresponding to each of our four clusters, rather than to the individual institutions.

To calculate expected admissions under each of our simulations, we simply multiply the projected number of test-takers at each SAT level by an estimated application rate to each type of school and then by an estimated admissions rate. Under the current regime both application rates and admissions rates differ by race. Under a race-neutral policy, blacks and whites with the same test scores would face the same probability of admission, conditional on application; we use observed white admissions rates (Figure 3) as a proxy for the race-blind admissions rule.[10]

A large shift in admissions probabilities would likely lead to responses in black students' decisions about where to apply. At each SAT score, black students are currently more likely than whites to apply to the most selective institutions. One might expect application rates to converge as admissions probabilities do. On the other hand, at least in the short run the elimination of race-conscious admission policies in Texas and California appears not to have altered the pattern of applications of high-achieving black students.[11] Our baseline estimates assume that race-specific application rates do not change, but we also consider a scenario in which black application rates come to resemble those of whites with similar scores.

Table 2 presents simulations based on the assumption that black application behavior remains as it is today. The first two rows repeat the actual black representation in 2000 and the simulated current race-blind representation from Table 1.[12] Row 3 applies the race-neutral admissions rule to the first counterfactual SAT distribution, assuming income convergence but no additional progress in test scores. This produces small gains in the representation of black students. Row 4 allows for projected reductions in the black–white test score gap among students with the same family income, on top of the impact of expected income convergence. This has a substantial effect on black representation.

---

10. If application behavior is unchanged, the elimination of racial preferences will reduce the total number of admittees. As the share of students admitted under affirmative action is small, this effect is as well. Nevertheless, to the extent that colleges lower the race-blind admissions standards to compensate, we will very slightly overestimate the effect of affirmative action on black admission shares.

11. David Card and Alan Krueger, "Would the Elimination of Affirmative Action Affect Highly Qualified Minority Applicants? Evidence from California and Texas," *Industrial and Labor Relations Review* 58, No. 3 (April 2005): 416–434.

12. Note that our analysis focuses on the number of admissions offers to black and white students. A single student may be admitted to several schools but can accept only one offer. We do not attempt to project changes in matriculation decisions.

Table 2. Projected black share of admitted students at elite institutions in 2025

	Most Selective	Highly Selective	Moderately Selective	Public
	Black share of admits			
Actual, 2000				
Status quo admissions rules	0.171	0.142	0.094	0.118
Race-blind admissions rules	0.051	0.060	0.051	0.053
Projected, 2025, with race-blind admissions				
Income growth only	0.069	0.078	0.062	0.064
Income plus test score growth	0.118	0.117	0.087	0.088
	Share of gap closed			
Actual, 2000				
Race-blind admissions rules	0.000	0.000	0.000	0.000
Projected, 2025, with race-blind admissions				
Income growth only	0.153	0.214	0.254	0.169
Income plus test score growth	0.557	0.700	0.835	0.545

For each type of college, we measure the distance to be covered as the gap between the current representation of black students and that which would be seen with race-neutral admissions, as in Table 1. For each projection, we then compute the share of this distance that is actually covered. Income convergence alone closes only about one-fifth of the gap. *It appears that reasonable income convergence will not, on its own, allow for the abolition of affirmative action without severely affecting the representation of African American students at elite colleges.* Additional progress on test scores will be required. Our estimates show that past experience will not be sufficient, at least at the public and most selective institutions: Even in our optimistic projections, only half of the gap is closed. (At the highly and moderately selective institutions, progress is more impressive but still insufficient to reproduce today's racial diversity.)

The estimates in Table 2 are predicated on the assumption that black application behavior will not change in response to the elimination of race-based preferences. We have also conducted the analysis under the alternative assumption that black application rates will come to resemble those of whites with the same test scores. This is decidedly more pessimistic, as many more high-scoring whites than blacks opt not to apply to the most selective colleges. The impact of a shift to race-blind admissions would then be much more dramatic, and projected future black representation at elite colleges would fall far short of that seen today.[13]

---

13. Krueger, Rothstein, and Turner, "Race, Income, and College in 25 Years."

Discussion

In an equal opportunity society, the effects of past discrimination on current generations will eventually asymptote to zero, though there is substantial uncertainty about the rate at which this might be expected to occur. In *Grutter v. Bollinger,* Justice O'Connor suggests rapid progress, enough so that the use of affirmative action to achieve diversity will be unnecessary within the next generation. Our simulations suggest that O'Connor's prediction is quite optimistic but not outside the realm of possibility.

We are most confident in predicting that economic progress alone will not yield as much racial diversity as is generated with today's race-sensitive admissions policies. Under plausible assumptions, black economic gains over the next quarter century can be expected to provide only about 17 percent of the incremental representation of African American students on elite college campuses that is provided by affirmative action today.

Our projections that also extrapolate past increases in black students' test scores relative to whites' are more hopeful. In this scenario, and if black college application behavior is assumed stable, we find that race-blind admissions policies may approach the black representation achieved by affirmative action, at least in some categories of colleges. This projection is likely overly optimistic: The last 25 years saw two distinct regimes, with rapidly closing black–white gaps in the first period and a widening gap since 1990. To extrapolate a linear trend a full quarter century into the future is to assume a dramatic turnaround from recent patterns and sustained growth over a long period. On the other hand, if we could somehow return to and sustain the rapid rate of progress seen in the 1980s, the future will be brighter than even our optimistic forecasts indicate.

As an indication of the difficulty of achieving racial diversity on highly selective college campuses without affirmative action, we have also considered the effects of a wholly implausible intervention producing the complete integration of the nation's secondary schools.[14] This, we estimate, would produce only a small fraction of the test score gains that would be needed to make Justice O'Connor's prediction a reality. Clearly, substantial progress in increasing black students' precollegiate performance is critical to any hope of eliminating the need for affirmative action within the next generation.

---

14. David Card and Jesse Rothstein ("Racial Segregation and the Black–White Test Score Gap," National Bureau of Economic Research, Working Paper #12078 [May 2005]) show that racial segregation has a negative effect on black students' performance. We almost certainly overstate the benefits of integration by assuming that it would equalize the contribution of schools to black and white students' achievement (Krueger, Rothstein, and Turner, "Race, Income, and College in 25 Years"). That even this indicates substantially smaller test score gains than are assumed in our primary analysis serves to underscore the optimism inherent in the latter.

Absent such progress, a shift to race-blind admissions in 25 years would lead to substantial declines in black representation at the nation's most selective colleges and universities. Our simulations, crude as they are, lead us to agree with Justice Ruth Bader Ginsburg's concurring opinion in *Grutter*: "From today's vantage point, one may hope, but not firmly forecast, that over the next generation's span, progress toward nondiscrimination and genuinely equal opportunity will make it safe to sunset affirmative action."

Section II:
"Do What You Can…
Where You Are"

Watch What We Do (and Not What We Say):
How Student Aid Awards Vary with Financial Need and Academic Merit

III

Michael S. McPherson and Morton Owen Schapiro[1]

A number of factors have contributed to the increased interest in financial aid over the past decade: Rates of return to higher education attendance are at or near record levels; inequality in the distribution of income and wealth is the greatest since the days of the Great Depression; colleges and universities have generally become more reliant on net tuition as a source of revenue; and patterns of postsecondary attendance suggest that some talented low-income students are increasingly enrolling at two-year schools as opposed to more costly public or private four-year institutions.

The level and distribution of student aid awards, and their changes over time, are of obvious relevance to the theme of this volume. One significant factor (though certainly not the only one) influencing enrollment decisions of disadvantaged students is their families' ability to finance college expenses. Financial aid awards from both institutions and governments are an important factor in determining those expenses. We know that the gap in enrollment rates between more- and less-advantaged students has been growing for a number of years,[2] and it is natural to wonder what sort of role changes in ability to pay have played in that trend.

Merit aid is not by any means a new phenomenon: Going back a hundred years or more, American colleges have often found it useful to rely on aid for both needy and meritorious students as means of pursuing their goals. (For a striking example, see Jonathan Reischl's paper on the role of financial aid in the early days of the University of Chicago.) In earlier work, we have focused on the rise of merit aid as a deliberate strategy in American colleges in the last several decades, a development that not only reflects the growing competitive pressures placed on colleges and universities, but also is in tension with the principle of pricing a college according

---

1. The authors thank Jonathan Reischl and Bibek Pandey for their superb research assistance. The idea to ignore need-based and merit labels and to instead let the data speak for themselves came from Bill Bowen, to whom we are always indebted.

2. Michael S. McPherson and Morton Owen Schapiro, "U.S. Higher Education Finance," in Eric Hanushek and Finis Welch, eds., *Handbook of the Economics of Education* (Amsterdam: Elsevier, forthcoming).

to a family's ability to pay.[3] Although it is commonplace to track the importance of merit as opposed to need-based aid based on the responses given by college and university administrators on survey forms, we have argued that the distinction between "need-based" and "non-need-based" student grants is a slippery one.

Many students who receive need-based assistance from a college will also receive a "merit award" (or "non-need" award) as part of their overall aid package. Sometimes such a merit award will boost a student's total grant dollars above those of another student with similar means who didn't receive a "merit" award; in other cases, the school may simply be putting a "merit" label on dollars the student would have gotten anyway. Similarly, two students at the same college, both receiving only need-based aid, may receive quite different aid packages. The more desirable student may receive either a larger total aid package or a similar package but with a larger component of grant aid and lower amounts of loans and work than the less desirable student receives. (A pioneering analysis of this strategic use of student aid was done by Ehrenberg and Sherman.[4]) And this can happen without any of the dollars being labeled "merit" dollars.

These ambiguities are understandable, since there is no obvious canonical definition of merit aid for colleges to rely on. Yet the lack of clarity may also arise in part from the fact that some schools are hesitant to be explicit about the extent to which they "buy students" through the aggressive use of merit packages, while others suspect that they get more bang for the buck by relabeling a scholarship based on need as one based on merit (Avery and Hoxby provide empirical evidence that these suspicions are in fact substantiated by student behavior.[5]) In this essay we take a different approach: We simply ignore the labels provided by colleges and universities and look directly at how financial aid grants vary with income, SATs, and other factors.

---

3. Michael S. McPherson and Morton Owen Schapiro, *Keeping College Affordable: Government and Educational Opportunity* (Washington, D.C.: The Brookings Institution, 1991); Michael S. McPherson and Morton Owen Schapiro, *The Student Aid Game: Meeting Need and Rewarding Talent in American Higher Education* (Princeton, N.J.: Princeton University Press, 1998); Michael S. McPherson and Morton Owen Schapiro, "Tracking the Impact of Academic 'Merit' on Need-based and Non-need-based Financial Aid Grants," unpublished paper (November 2001); and Michael S. McPherson and Morton Owen Schapiro, "The Blurring Line Between Merit and Need in Financial Aid," *Change* 34, No. 2 (March/April 2002): 38–46.

4. Ronald Ehrenberg and Daniel Sherman, "Optimal Financial Aid Policies for a Selective University, *Journal of Human Resources* (Spring 1984): 202–230.

5. Christopher Avery and Caroline M. Hoxby, "Do and Should Financial Aid Packages Affect Students' College Choices?" in *College Choices: The Economics of Where to Go, When to Go, and How to Pay for It*, Caroline M. Hoxby, editor, National Bureau of Economic Research Conference Report (Chicago: University of Chicago Press, 2004).

For some years now, the U.S. Department of Education has been conducting a periodic survey of a broadly representative random sample of college students, measuring carefully how they and their families meet the cost of the colleges they attend. The data we focus on are for full-time, dependent undergraduate students attending four-year, nonprofit colleges and universities as reported in the National Postsecondary Student Aid Survey (NPSAS) in 1992–1993 and in 1999–2000. Data are obtained from the students, from the institutional record, and (for a subsample) from parents. In our data, athletic grants-in-aid are excluded from our student aid grant calculations.

Tables 1, 2, and 3 allow us to describe in summary form the amounts of grant aid students differing in family income and SAT scores received in 1992–1993 and 1999–2000. Table 1 presents grant totals broken down by family income and by individual student SAT scores in 1999–2000 dollar values. SAT scores (which here are adjusted for recentering) are used as a convenient measure of academic achievement and promise that can be readily compared across students. We distinguish between grants that are awarded directly by institutions (using either their own funds or federal money [SEOG, Supplemental Educational Opportunity Grants, which are awarded on a discretionary basis by schools]) and all grants (which include Pell dollars and state grants awarded directly to students).

Beginning with institutionally awarded grants, it is clear that at both public and private colleges and universities family income has a significant impact on financial aid, as one would expect in a system built at least in part around family ability to pay. In each of the survey years, controlling broadly for SAT scores, students in the lowest income group receive more grant aid than those in the highest income group. Moreover, with certain exceptions, grants rise consistently as incomes fall.

The important exception to this rule is for low SAT students attending private colleges and universities, where institutionally awarded grants are higher for middle-income than for low-income students in both 1992–1993 and in 1999–2000.

However, the pattern changes over time. In 1992–1993, at private colleges and universities, low-income students within a particular SAT range received much more institutionally awarded grant aid than those in the highest income group—6.5 times in the lowest SAT group, 3.5 times in the middle SAT group, and 4.9 times in the highest SAT group. By 1999–2000, those multiples had fallen to 1.1 times, 2.2 times, and 2.8 times. While income seems to play a smaller role in the allocation of grants at private institutions in the more recent year, SAT scores continue to play a large role. In 1992–1993, low-income/high SAT students received 4.9 times as much institutionally awarded grant aid as their low SAT counterparts, a figure that fell to a still substantial 3.9 times in 1999–2000. For

Table 1. Grant aid by income and SAT, 1992–1993 and 1999–2000, in 1999–2000 dollars

	SAT	High	Upper Middle	Middle	Low
All grants					
Private Colleges and Universities					
Income level					
1992–1993	Low	609	1417	3997	5222
	Middle	1579	2032	5402	8269
	High	1663	3852	7326	10846
1999–2000	Low	2424	3936	4825	5901
	Middle	2336	4077	5815	8801
	High	3509	6374	9643	12290
Public Colleges and Universities					
Income level					
1992–1993	Low	5	259	961	1890
	Middle	172	266	910	1741
	High	424	487	1312	2450
1999–2000	Low	356	262	1343	3619
	Middle	263	351	1247	3904
	High	663	890	1854	3535
Institutionally awarded grants (includes SEOG)					
Private Colleges and Universities					
Income level					
1992–1993	Low	253	1135	2442	1645
	Middle	1509	1902	4200	5348
	High	1645	3659	6556	8134
1999–2000	Low	2210	3177	3529	2470
	Middle	2198	3556	4311	4889
	High	3400	6113	8336	9541
Public Colleges and Universities					
Income level					
1992–1993	Low	5	148	371	550
	Middle	95	182	417	471
	High	274	331	703	669
1999–2000	Low	291	110	357	508
	Middle	159	174	425	775
	High	546	618	940	1292

SAT categories: High—above 1100, Middle—900–1100, Low—below 900.
Income categories: High—above $100,000, Upper Middle—$60,000–$100,000,
Middle—$30,000–$60,000, Low—below $30,000.

Table 2. Discount rates for public and private colleges and universities, 1992–1993 and 1999–2000

Discount rate (all grants)					
Private Colleges and Universities					
Income Level					
	SAT	High	Upper Middle	Middle	Low
1992–1993	Low	5.2%	11.1%	36.5%	58.9%
	Middle	10.3%	13.5%	38.3%	61.6%
	High	9.3%	21.6%	43.0%	61.8%
1999–2000	Low	17.7%	28.5%	34.5%	57.7%
	Middle	13.9%	25.7%	39.1%	61.0%
	High	17.1%	32.4%	49.6%	67.3%
Public Colleges and Universities					
Income level					
	SAT	High	Upper Middle	Middle	Low
1992–1993	Low	0.1%	7.1%	24.6%	62.2%
	Middle	4.4%	7.0%	25.9%	51.6%
	High	7.8%	10.4%	31.1%	70.0%
1999–2000	Low	7.1%	6.3%	31.5%	93.0%
	Middle	5.3%	7.5%	28.3%	92.8%
	High	11.3%	16.7%	38.5%	80.8%
Discount rate (institutionally awarded grants)					
Private Colleges and Universities					
Income Level					
	SAT	High	Upper Middle	Middle	Low
1992–1993	Low	2.2%	8.9%	22.3%	18.6%
	Middle	9.8%	12.6%	29.8%	39.9%
	High	9.2%	20.6%	38.4%	46.3%
1999–2000	Low	16.1%	23.0%	25.2%	24.1%
	Middle	13.1%	22.4%	29.0%	33.9%
	High	16.6%	31.1%	42.3%	52.2%
Public Colleges and Universities					
Income level					
	SAT	High	Upper Middle	Middle	Low
1992–1993	Low	0.1%	4.1%	9.5%	15.7%
	Middle	2.4%	4.8%	11.9%	14.0%
	High	5.0%	7.0%	16.7%	22.0%
1999–2000	Low	5.8%	2.6%	8.4%	13.1%
	Middle	3.2%	3.7%	9.7%	18.4%
	High	9.3%	11.6%	19.5%	29.5%

Table 3. Net tuition in public and private colleges and universities, 1992–1993 and 1999–2000, in 1999–2000 dollars

		Private Colleges and Universities			
		Income Level			
	SAT	High	Upper Middle	Middle	Low
	Low	11011	11310	6955	3636
1992–1993	Middle	13751	13038	8705	5149
	High	16189	13948	9724	6717
	Low	11296	9871	9164	4331
1999–2000	Middle	14412	11765	9039	5626
	High	17067	13309	9812	5978
		Public Colleges and Universities			
		Income level			
	SAT	High	Upper Middle	Middle	Low
	Low	3667	3376	2941	1149
1992–1993	Middle	3735	3536	2603	1636
	High	5038	4212	2903	1049
	Low	4644	3911	2926	271
1999–2000	Middle	4681	4350	3157	303
	High	5208	4448	2963	838

middle-income students, the change in multiples was even smaller—from 2.7 times to 2.3 times.

In each of the years, institutionally awarded grants at private colleges and universities are largest for the lowest income/highest SAT students, a fact that many higher-education observers would undoubtedly endorse. When we add Pell and state grants to the mix, low-income/high SAT students again receive the largest grants but, given the income sensitivity of Pell Grants, income becomes a more important factor than when grants are limited to those awarded directly by institutions. Note that when Pell and state grants are included, low-income/low SAT students at private institutions do receive larger awards than middle-income students, suggesting that the colleges take the presence of Pell into account in deciding how to allocate their own grant awards.

As with institutionally awarded grants, income becomes somewhat less important over time for all grants as well, with multiples falling from 8.6 times, 5.2 times, and 6.5 times in 1992–1993 to 2.4 times, 3.8 times, and 3.5 times in 1999–2000.

The scene at public colleges and universities has similarities to and differences from what we observe at private institutions. Whether looking at all grants or just institutionally awarded grants, there is a less systematic relationship among awards, income, and SAT scores. Although there is a generally negative relationship between family income and award level, only for all grants in 1992–1993 and for institutionally awarded grants in 1999–2000 is it even the case that low-income/high SAT students receive the largest amount of aid. Table 1 does, however, document a generally positive relationship between SAT scores and award levels at public institutions.

Table 2 has the same format as Table 1, but this time we look at the discount rate off the sticker price—in other words, the percentage of tuition a student in a particular income/SAT group actually receives as grants. In every case but one (all grants at public colleges and universities in 1999–2000), the largest discount an institution provides is for low-income/high SAT students. Discounts at private colleges and universities generally increased over time, with the largest increases going to more affluent students. The picture is more mixed at public institutions.

From the viewpoint not of institutional revenues but of affordability, the "all grants" part of the table is of most interest. There we see that discounts off sticker prices at private colleges and universities were largest for the lowest income students and these discounts changed little over time (59, 62, and 62 percent in 1992–1993 to 58, 61, and 67 percent in 1999–2000). At public colleges and universities, discounts for low-income students rose quite a bit for all SAT groups (from 62, 52 and 70 percent to 93, 93 and 81 percent). Of course, an increase in the price discount does not mean that net prices actually fell. When grant aid increases at a faster rate than the sticker price, the discount rate rises even when the absolute gap between the sticker price and the grant award grows. What low-income students and their parents care about is the net price they face and the empirical literature suggests that their higher education attendance is quite responsive to changes in price.[6]

Table 3 provides data on price net of all grants. While low-income students in the low and middle SAT groups who attended private colleges and universities experienced real increases in net prices, their high SAT counterparts faced a reduction in real net tuition. For low-income students attending public institutions, real net tuition fell across the board. The pattern for more affluent students is mixed. Middle- and high-income students attending private colleges and universities experienced real price increases while upper-middle-income students at privates experienced a real decline in the prices they faced. The decline

---

6. For example, see McPherson and Schapiro, *Keeping College Affordable*; and Thomas J. Kane, *The Price of Admission: Rethinking How Americans Pay for College* (Washington, D.C.: The Brookings Institution, 1999).

In real prices for low-income students at public institutions was not replicated among students from other income groups who, in all but one case, experienced increases in real net prices.

The finding about low-income students is of particular interest. Substantial increases in Pell Grants accompanied by some increase in state grants for low-income students actually resulted in a fall in the price net of grants that public university and college students faced. It is of interest that this drop in net price, which was not shared by other income groups at public institutions, apparently was not enough to reverse the growing gap in enrollment between low-income and more affluent students.

It is perilous to read too much into the tabular analysis in these tables given the lack of any controls other than broad ones for SAT scores and income. Our data show, for example, that at private colleges and universities part of the difference in grants between students with higher and lower SAT scores comes from the fact that students with high scores attend more expensive institutions. In fact, in some of our earlier work[7] we examined data on SAT scores, income, and aid awards separately for students at high-tuition and low-tuition institutions. Not surprisingly, at private institutions, the positive relationship between SAT scores and grant aid was reduced with even this crude control for tuition, indicating that some of the additional grant aid for high SAT students resulted from the presence of these students at particularly expensive private colleges and universities. At public institutions, however, the relationship between the SAT score and grant aid was less affected, reflecting a weaker relationship between average SAT scores and the tuition level at public universities than at private ones. Instead, much of the variation in public tuition is explained by variation in state tuition policies rather than by differences in institutional prestige or "quality."

This tabular analysis is suggestive, but it requires stronger statistical verification, a task to which we now turn.

Econometric Results

The data described in the previous section provide a rich description of how grant aid is distributed across students with varying family income backgrounds and SAT scores. However, we know that the observed variation is a product of a variety of factors that may differ across different groups of students classified by test scores and family resources. On average, as just discussed, students from

---

7. Michael S. McPherson and Morton Owen Schapiro, "The Blurring Line Between Merit and Need in Financial Aid," *Change* 34, No. 2 (March/April 2002: 38–46).

more affluent families generally attend more expensive colleges and universities. Levels of grant aid, in turn, are likely to be correlated with tuition levels. There is also likely to be systematic variation concerning the types of institutions students from different groups attend, and race and gender may also be related to levels of grant awards. What we would like to know is how grant awards vary with SAT scores and family income *after* controlling for such other factors influencing these awards, including institutional factors such as tuition levels and institutional type as well as personal factors including gender and race-ethnic background.

The obvious way to account for such multiple sources of variation is through a multivariate statistical analysis. This is the approach we follow here, estimating equations that seek to explain observed variations in grant award levels as a function of the variables named in the preceding paragraph. Most readers will be familiar with a technique for doing this called "multiple regression," which permits one to estimate the degree of relationship between two variables while holding the values of other variables constant. A complication for us is that multiple regression relies on the assumption that the dependent variable (grant award size in our case) can take on any value. But no one receives a grant below zero and, in fact, a significant fraction of the students we observe have grant levels of zero. We therefore employ a variant of multiple regression called "Tobit analysis," which takes account of the fact that the value of grant awards has many observations at zero. The interpretation of the relationships estimated in this Tobit analysis differs in subtle but significant ways from multiple regression. For the sake of expositional simplicity, we will not go into detail on these complexities here, but they are described more fully in a version of this paper available on the Spencer Foundation Web site.

Explaining Variation in Grant Awards with a Tobit Analysis

We seek to explain variation in the two variables described earlier: institutionally awarded grants (coming from cither school funds or SEOG dollars) and all grants (which add Pell and state financial aid grants to the institutionally awarded figure).

We examine the relationship between each of these grant measures and a set of independent variables that includes level of financial need, SAT score, tuition level, Carnegie classification of institution, gender, and race. The aim is to clarify as well as we can the observed relationship among ability to pay, academic preparation, and grant award levels while removing the influence of confounding factors like variation in tuition levels and the like. Please understand that we are not claiming to isolate a causal relationship among variables—we cannot for example claim that if a particular student were to have raised her SAT score by X points the college she is attending would have increased her financial aid award by Y dollars. All we can observe is the "equilibrium" structure that existed at a given point in time, a structure that is the joint outcome of decisions by students about which colleges to apply to, by colleges about what kind of financial aid offers to make, and by students about which offers to accept. Our aim is to provide an illuminating description of these "equilibrium relationships" as they existed in two different years, after filtering out the influence of other related factors on aid awards, not to explain them causally.

A full set of Tobit equations for our two dependent variables (all grants and institutionally awarded grants) for the two academic years (1992–1993 and 1999–2000) and for the two institutional groups (private colleges/universities and public colleges/universities) is reported in Tables 5–8. Most of our analyses will focus on the two variables of particular interest, EFC and SAT, and in Table 4 we provide the Tobit coefficients and standard errors for these variables from each of the eight estimated equations. Before turning to those findings, we will review briefly the full equations reported in these tables.

"Need" or "ability to pay" in all of the equations is measured by the Expected Family Contribution (EFC). This variable, which is constructed by the National Center for Education Statistics from data items in their *National Postsecondary Student Aid Study* (NPSAS) survey, aims to replicate the key variable in determining family ability to pay for college in the federal needs-analysis system. This system assumes that a percentage of family income and assets should be available for paying for college, after adjusting for factors like the need to save for retirement, the number of children in the family, and a variety of other items. We think it is a better variable for measuring family ability to pay than family income because the EFC variable

Table 4. Tobit coefficients and standard errors

		Institutionally awarded grants			
		Private Coefficient	**SE**	**Public Coefficient**	**SE**
1992–1993	EFC	-0.33	0.015	-0.08	0.01
	SAT	7.25	0.789	3.15	0.461
1999–2000	EFC	-0.24	0.012	-0.11	0.009
	SAT	8.66	0.968	6.48	0.575
		All grants			
		Private Coefficient	**SE**	**Public Coefficient**	**SE**
1992–1993	EFC	-0.38	0.015	-0.16	0.009
	SAT	6.12	0.788	2.18	0.417
1999–2000	EFC	-0.29	0.012	-0.19	0.008
	SAT	7.22	0.974	3.34	0.49

takes into account accumulated assets and several relevant features of family circumstances.[8] As expected, the sign on EFC (which, of course, varies inversely with need) is negative and less than one in all equations and is highly significant statistically. That is to say, a one-dollar increase in family ability to pay is associated with a less than one-dollar decrease in grant aid awarded in all of our estimates.

We use the SAT as our measure of academic accomplishment and promise, both because it is readily available in the data and because it can be compared more meaningfully across students than can a variable like high school GPA. As expected, the sign on SAT is positive and the relationship is estimated with considerable precision. Students with higher SAT scores reliably receive larger grant awards, after controlling for other factors.

Turning to other explanatory variables, the regressions in Tables 5–8 show that *tuition* is also positively related to the amount of grant aid awarded, with a coefficient less than one. That is, with other things being equal, a student at an institution with higher tuition will tend to receive a higher grant aid award that partially offsets the higher tuition. A coefficient greater than one would imply that, on average, net tuition would be negatively related to gross tuition, which would be a surprising result.

The coefficients on the race/ethnicity variables show how grant aid awards vary with racial category, as compared to the omitted category of white students. In most, but not all, of the equations, *black* and *Hispanic* students receive larger grant awards, with other things being equal, than white students, while no other groups show any consistent, statistically significant relationship. This may reflect competitive pressures to recruit students of color, or possibly it may indicate that our measure of need does not adequately account for the impact of the weak asset position of minority group members on their ability to pay.

There is some evidence that gender makes a difference to award levels, with women receiving somewhat larger awards than men.

The next set of variables distinguishes among types of institution, by Carnegie Classification.[9] The values in the tables show grant awards at different

8. Equations with family income substituted for EFC yield qualitatively similar results. Notice that, for a single college that fully met the need of all students with grants, we would expect the coefficient on EFC to be negative one for students whose need (the difference between cost of attendance and EFC) was greater than zero and zero for all students whose need was zero or less.

9. We use the 1994 definition of the classification, which includes two classes of research universities, two classes of other doctorate-granting universities, two classes of comprehensive or master's-granting universities, two classes of baccalaureate institutions (liberal arts college are baccalaureate I and others are baccalaureate II), and a variety of specialized institution types. See http://www.carnegiefoundation.org/Classification/CIHE2000/background.htm (Web site visited May 30, 2005).

Table 5. Private colleges and universities: 1992–1993

Institutionally awarded grants						
Tobit estimates				Number of obs	=	2440
				LR chi2 (20)	=	771.54
				Prob > chi2	=	0.0000
Log likelihood = -14213.761				Pseudo R2	=	0.0264
Install	**Coef.**	**Std. Err.**	**t**	**P>|t|**	**[95% Conf. Interval]**	
EFC	-.3295292	.0149732	-22.01	0.000	-.3588908	-.3001677
SAT	7.253453	.7888458	9.20	0.000	5.706571	8.800336
Tuition	.3338304	.0380548	8.77	0.000	.2592071	.4084538
Black	135.2069	517.9092	0.26	0.794	-880.3843	1150.798
Hispanic	445.4369	552.1032	0.81	0.420	-637.2069	1528.081
Asian	65.92898	627.3031	0.11	0.916	-1164.178	1296.036
Natamer	-1669.76	2384.156	-0.70	0.484	-6344.958	3005.437
Female	592.1954	254.3433	2.33	0.020	93.44227	1090.949
RES2	2543.493	647.0818	3.93	0.000	1274.602	3812.385
DOC1	1293.506	602.5411	2.15	0.032	111.9561	2475.056
DOC2	1474.698	657.5679	2.24	0.025	185.2432	2764.152
MAS1	1639.196	503.6201	3.25	0.001	651.6579	2626.733
MAS2	3964.329	864.279	4.59	0.000	2269.526	5659.133
BAC1	1786.971	428.9294	4.17	0.000	945.8644	2628.078
BAC2	2303.618	560.7971	4.11	0.000	1203.926	3403.31
Seminary	-1770.395	3976.846	-0.45	0.656	-9568.77	6027.98
Health	-2352.937	1245.036	-1.89	0.059	-4794.385	88.51003
Engineer	-6016.345	3038.33	-1.98	0.048	-11974.34	-58.34839
Business	2411.843	1203.903	2.00	0.045	51.05582	4772.631
Art	4979.905	1346.576	3.70	0.000	2339.345	7620.466
_cons	-9130.235	1144.598	-7.98	0.000	-11374.73	-6885.74
_se	5502.603	114.8724		(Ancillary parameter)		
1091 left-censored observations at install<=0; 1349 uncensored observations						

All grants						
Tobit estimates				Number of obs	=	2440
				LR chi2(20)	=	896.01
				Prob > chi2	=	0.0000
Log likelihood = -15557.55				Pseudo R2	=	0.0280
All	**Coef.**	**Std. Err.**	**t**	**P>|t|**	**[95% Conf. Interval]**	
EFC	-.3765009	.014969	-25.15	0.000	-.4058541	-.3471476
SAT	6.123538	.7876014	7.77	0.000	4.579095	7.667981
Tuition	.2368652	.0378248	6.26	0.000	.1626929	.3110376
Black	1230.251	506.4915	2.43	0.015	237.0488	2223.452
Hispanic	1596.642	544.3809	2.93	0.003	529.1417	2664.143
Asian	573.2803	629.051	0.91	0.362	-660.2538	1806.814
Natamer	-2082.135	2437.283	-0.85	0.393	-6861.512	2697.242
Female	481.7786	254.9597	1.89	0.059	-18.18326	981.7405
RES2	2373.353	655.4396	3.62	0.000	1088.072	3658.634
DOC1	1139.146	604.4474	1.88	0.060	-46.14208	2324.434
DOC2	1262.798	666.7302	1.89	0.058	-44.62344	2570.219
MAS1	1547.939	503.9554	3.07	0.002	559.71	2536.167
MAS2	3256.149	874.5594	3.72	0.000	1541.186	4971.111
BAC1	1785.628	432.4787	4.13	0.000	937.5608	2633.694
BAC2	2248.645	562.0464	4.00	0.000	1146.503	3350.787
Seminary	562.5523	3300.452	0.17	0.865	-5909.451	7034.555
Health	-1116.202	1218.934	-0.92	0.360	-3506.464	1274.06
Engineer	-4873.962	2407.557	-2.02	0.043	-9595.049	-152.8748
Business	1585.474	1214.781	1.31	0.192	-796.6438	3967.591
Art	4445.451	1368.907	3.25	0.001	1761.101	7129.802
_cons	-5117.962	1137.582	-4.50	0.000	-7348.698	-2887.226
_se	5614.376	110.5213		(Ancillary parameter)		
954 left-censored observations at all<=0; 1486 uncensored observations						

Table 6. Public colleges and universities: 1992–1993

Institutionally awarded grants						
Tobit estimates				Number of obs	=	2917
				LR chi2(17)	=	249.79
				Prob > chi2	=	0.0000
Log likelihood = -6504.5065				Pseudo R2	=	0.0188
Install	**Coef.**	**Std. Err.**	**t**	**P>|t|**	**[95% Conf.**	**Interval]**
EFC	-.0836843	.0095745	-8.74	0.000	-.1024579	-.0649107
SAT	3.148521	.4610149	6.83	0.000	2.244571	4.052471
Tuition	.1653278	.0302757	5.46	0.000	.1059637	.2246918
Black	1461.921	297.1515	4.92	0.000	879.2716	2044.571
Hispanic	1278.677	296.9763	4.31	0.000	696.3712	1860.983
Asian	577.1025	370.2748	1.56	0.119	-148.9256	1303.131
Natamer	870.2342	1003.441	0.87	0.386	-1097.294	2837.763
Female	470.8321	160.8357	2.93	0.003	155.4683	786.196
RES2	-147.7663	299.5449	-0.49	0.622	-735.1087	439.5761
DOC1	394.3045	370.4127	1.06	0.287	-331.9941	1120.603
DOC2	-687.6719	478.6555	-1.44	0.151	-1626.211	250.8672
MAS1	-666.878	199.4057	-3.34	0.001	-1057.869	-275.8868
MAS2	272.0557	399.7125	0.68	0.496	-511.6935	1055.805
BAC1	1400.673	1056.565	1.33	0.185	-671.0211	3472.367
BAC2	407.3657	426.2161	0.96	0.339	-428.3512	1243.083
ASSC	-14731.94	.	.	.	.	.
Art	101.4646	1401.472	0.07	0.942	-2646.516	2849.445
_cons	-5807.887	556.4968	-10.44	0.000	-6899.056	-4716.718
_se	3014.813	99.96792	(Ancillary parameter)			
2310 left-censored observations at install<=0; 607 uncensored observations						
All grants						
Tobit estimates				Number of obs	=	2917
				LR chi2(17)	=	534.42
				Prob > chi2	=	0.0000
Log likelihood = -10641.821				Pseudo R2	=	0.0245
All	**Coef.**	**Std. Err.**	**t**	**P>|t|**	**[95% Conf.**	**Interval]**
EFC	-.1576627	.0094494	-16.68	0.000	-.1761909	-.1391345
SAT	2.176674	.4173693	5.22	0.000	1.358304	2.995045
Tuition	.148827	.0287524	5.18	0.000	.0924498	.2052043
Black	2037.827	263.4394	7.74	0.000	1521.279	2554.374
Hispanic	1572.172	273.8441	5.74	0.000	1035.224	2109.121
Asian	311.7241	353.0101	0.88	0.377	-380.4519	1003.9
Natamer	1403.699	870.2434	1.61	0.107	-302.659	3110.057
Female	252.5603	145.0153	1.74	0.082	-31.78305	536.9037
RES2	-332.1421	275.5974	-1.21	0.228	-872.5286	208.2444
DOC1	-322.3555	361.7257	-0.89	0.373	-1031.621	386.9098
DOC2	-261.3475	409.74	-0.64	0.524	-1064.758	542.0634
MAS1	-323.5929	177.7603	-1.82	0.069	-672.1422	24.9564
MAS2	73.78137	372.6429	0.20	0.843	-656.8902	804.453
BAC1	1069.854	1030.931	1.04	0.299	-951.5759	3091.285
BAC2	580.6318	393.0193	1.48	0.140	-189.9936	1351.257
ASSC	-17795.15	.	.	.	.	.
Art	-4.286001	1294.437	-0.00	0.997	-2542.396	2533.824
_cons	-2689.471	485.4025	-5.54	0.000	-3641.24	-1737.702
_se	3122.359	77.90022	(Ancillary parameter)			
1887 left-censored observations at all<=0; 1030 uncensored observations						

Table 7. Private colleges and universities. 1999‑2000

Institutionally awarded grants						
Tobit estimates				Number of obs	=	3175
				LR chi2(21)	=	635.64
				Prob > chi2	=	0.0000
Log likelihood = -21862.654				Pseudo R2	=	0.0143
Install	**Coef.**	**Std. Err.**	**t**	**P>|t|**	**[95% Conf. Interval]**	
EFC	-.236653	.0115686	-20.46	0.000	-.2593358	-.2139702
SAT	8.655071	.9684815	8.94	0.000	6.756154	10.55399
Tuition	.262314	.0338766	7.74	0.000	.1958915	.3287365
Black	2056.63	620.9588	3.31	0.001	839.1061	3274.154
Hispanic	209.6103	584.763	0.36	0.720	-936.944	1356.165
Asian	-11.24672	742.4225	-0.02	0.988	-1466.927	1444.433
Natamer	-601.3606	2115.991	-0.28	0.776	-4750.219	3547.498
Pacisland	396.6519	1724.2	0.23	0.818	-2984.015	3777.319
Other	-1283.514	1289.03	-1.00	0.319	-3810.935	1243.908
Female	959.7093	298.604	3.21	0.001	374.2317	1545.187
RES2	1385.017	710.5982	1.95	0.051	-8.264513	2778.299
DOC1	1992.335	694.8229	2.87	0.004	629.984	3354.685
DOC2	-1857.596	828.0543	-2.24	0.025	-3481.175	-234.0161
MAS1	2250.51	548.7338	4.10	0.000	1174.598	3326.421
MAS2	3195.559	852.0143	3.75	0.000	1525	4866.117
BAC1	847.2374	532.4397	1.59	0.112	-196.7258	1891.201
BAC2	3325.059	601.1361	5.53	0.000	2146.401	4503.716
Seminary	415.7203	1725.804	0.24	0.810	-2968.092	3799.532
Engineer	-48623.34	.	.	.	.	.
Business	-2078.157	1244.534	-1.67	0.095	-4518.335	362.0218
Art	-1727.01	1314.97	-1.31	0.189	-4305.292	851.2724
_cons	-10367.89	1438.028	-7.21	0.000	-13187.46	-7548.326
_se	7646.952	129.5711		(Ancillary parameter)		
1150 left-censored observations at install<=0; 2025 uncensored observations						

All grants						
Tobit estimates				Number of obs	=	3175
				LR chi2(21)	=	795.39
				Prob > chi2	=	0.0000
Log likelihood = -23398.837				Pseudo R2	=	0.0167
All	**Coef.**	**Std. Err.**	**t**	**P>|t|**	**[95% Conf. Interval]**	
EFC	-.2938572	.011852	-24.79	0.000	-.3170955	-.2706189
SAT	7.216415	.9740169	7.41	0.000	5.306644	9.126186
Tuition	.2094206	.033798	6.20	0.000	.1431523	.2756889
Black	2830.941	620.5702	4.56	0.000	1614.178	4047.703
Hispanic	1607.683	579.9554	2.77	0.006	470.5547	2744.811
Asian	923.2745	748.1916	1.23	0.217	-540.7100	2390.266
Natamer	-984.9567	2161.019	-0.46	0.649	-5222.103	3252.189
Pacisland	1250.855	1728.344	0.72	0.469	-2137.938	4639.647
Other	-821.2971	1297.869	-0.63	0.527	-3366.051	1723.456
Female	991.4357	300.8426	3.30	0.001	401.5686	1581.303
RES2	953.1883	721.4131	1.32	0.187	-461.2982	2367.675
DOC1	1784.753	701.476	2.54	0.011	409.3578	3160.149
DOC2	-1830.622	828.9388	-2.21	0.027	-3455.936	-205.3084
MAS1	1973.343	552.3479	3.57	0.000	890.3452	3056.34
MAS2	3116.494	856.5991	3.64	0.000	1436.946	4796.042
BAC1	535.8656	539.4159	0.99	0.321	-521.776	1593.507
BAC2	3235.042	604.6715	5.35	0.000	2049.452	4420.631
Seminary	-445.6742	1714.238	-0.26	0.795	-3806.809	2915.46
Engineer	-11581.02	3283.607	-3.53	0.000	-18019.24	-5142.797
Business	-1126.838	1190.507	-0.95	0.344	-3461.084	1207.409
Art	-1688.985	1305.731	-1.29	0.196	-4249.153	871.1836
_cons	-5738.379	1436.925	-3.99	0.000	-8555.781	-2920.977
_se	7788.277	125.8852		(Ancillary parameter)		
997 left-censored observations at all<=0; 2178 uncensored observations						

Table 8. Public colleges and universities: 1999–2000

Institutionally awarded grants						
Tobit estimates				Number of obs	=	4222
				LR chi2(19)	=	457.94
				Prob > chi2	=	0.0000
Log likelihood = -10665.982				Pseudo R2	=	0.0210
Install	**Coef.**	**Std. Err.**	**t**	**P>|t|**	**[95% Conf. Interval]**	
EFC	-.1098143	.0089653	-12.25	0.000	-.1273909	-.0922377
SAT	6.47591	.5749302	11.26	0.000	5.348743	7.603077
Tuition	.1745179	.026122	6.68	0.000	.1233051	.2257308
Black	2219.675	318.2418	6.97	0.000	1595.753	2843.597
Hispanic	1645.263	329.5328	4.99	0.000	999.2044	2291.321
Asian	1322.846	342.6547	3.86	0.000	651.0614	1994.63
Natamer	-2336.212	2244.189	-1.04	0.298	-6736.009	2063.585
Pacisland	-358.9073	1056.457	-0.34	0.734	-2430.121	1712.306
Other	1812.881	698.3013	2.60	0.009	443.8411	3181.92
Female	245.8929	179.8862	1.37	0.172	-106.779	598.5649
RES2	1380.259	294.4285	4.69	0.000	803.0239	1957.495
DOC1	509.4309	366.7116	1.39	0.165	-209.5177	1228.379
DOC2	245.7177	365.2667	0.67	0.501	-470.398	961.8334
MAS1	-506.9804	227.8072	-2.23	0.026	-953.603	-60.35785
MAS2	299.9147	580.8454	0.52	0.606	-838.8492	1438.679
BAC1	675.126	1293.058	0.52	0.602	-1859.951	3210.203
BAC2	-218.0137	815.8912	-0.27	0.789	-1817.592	1381.564
ASSC	-705.9301	1487.663	-0.47	0.635	-3622.535	2210.675
Art	2218.555	1284.861	1.73	0.084	-300.4523	4737.562
_cons	-10529.97	745.7754	-14.12	0.000	-11992.09	-9067.86
_se	4136.059	106.8102			(Ancillary parameter)	
3247 left-censored observations at install<=0; 975 uncensored observations						
All grants						
Tobit estimates				Number of obs	=	4222
				LR chi2(19)	=	876.47
				Prob > chi2	=	0.0000
Log likelihood = -17777.502				Pseudo R2	=	0.0241
All	**Coef.**	**Std. Err.**	**t**	**P>|t|**	**[95% Conf. Interval]**	
EFC	-.1900694	.0081341	-23.37	0.000	-.2060166	-.1741223
SAT	3.342887	.4900903	6.82	0.000	2.382051	4.303722
Tuition	.0520998	.0242139	2.15	0.031	.0046277	.0995718
Black	2404.893	274.389	8.76	0.000	1866.946	2942.841
Hispanic	1513.816	291.9126	5.19	0.000	941.5127	2086.119
Asian	1626.762	313.0144	5.20	0.000	1013.089	2240.436
Natamer	-2459.641	1851.625	-1.33	0.184	-6089.805	1170.522
Pacisland	200.2809	829.0331	0.24	0.809	-1425.062	1825.624
Other	938.4722	657.4367	1.43	0.154	-350.4512	2227.396
Female	461.7814	156.9307	2.94	0.003	154.1144	769.4484
RES2	753.8394	271.7303	2.77	0.006	221.1045	1286.574
DOC1	112.308	329.9626	0.34	0.734	-534.5932	759.2091
DOC2	-441.8014	325.9611	-1.36	0.175	-1080.857	197.2546
MAS1	-467.9625	193.8684	-2.41	0.016	-848.0471	-87.8779
MAS2	-390.3878	502.7867	-0.78	0.438	-1376.115	595.3398
BAC1	-299.7202	1191.991	-0.25	0.801	-2636.653	2037.213
BAC2	-580.9156	655.7177	-0.89	0.376	-1866.469	704.6377
ASSC	1417.982	1126.103	1.26	0.208	-789.7744	3625.738
Art	369.979	1221.598	0.30	0.762	-2025	2764.957
_cons	-3287.004	616.0681	-5.34	0.000	-4494.823	-2079.185
_se	4136.215	79.4207	(Ancillary parameter)			
2532 left-censored observations at all<=0; 1690 uncensored observations						

types of institutions compared to awards at research 1 institutions, which are generally the leading research universities in public and private higher education. These coefficients, which are in many cases not significant or not stable across equations, suggest that award levels do not vary systematically across institution types once you control for factors like the ability to pay, the academic credentials of their students, their tuition levels, and so on. However, one rather striking set of relationships does persist. In private higher education, both in 1999–2000 and in 1992–1993, master's-level and baccalaureate-level institutions tend to have higher award levels for their students than leading research institutions. This is particularly true of the master's II and baccalaureate II institutions, where the coefficients are quite large in dollar terms. Presumably, in addition to having lower tuition than research 1 institutions, these institutions, on average, need to provide students with more grant aid in order to attract students. The estimates are not precise enough to allow us to judge whether this difference has grown or declined between 1992–1993 and 1999–2000.

Some of the relationships shown in these tables are worthy of study in their own right, but for our purposes their main role is to allow us to focus on the role of the variables of central interest to us: ability to pay (EFC) and academic preparation (SAT). Thus, these equations allow us to examine the relationship between the level of grant aid that students receive, on the one hand, and their need levels and SAT scores, on the other, while controlling for the influence of other variables.[10]

We turn now to these results, which are summarized in Table 4. The coefficient on EFC in the all grants, private college and university equation for 1992–1993 is –.38. This indicates that as family ability to pay grows, grant awards fall by less than the amount of the increase in ability to pay. This coefficient can be found in the lower panel of Table 5 and is reproduced in Table 4, where all the SAT and EFC coefficients are summarized. (For quantitative estimates of the size of these effects, see the next section.) The SAT coefficient of 6.12 indicates that higher SAT scores are associated with higher grant award levels. These coefficients are significantly different from zero (as are all the coefficients in Table 4), as indicated by the fact that the standard errors are in every case considerably less than half the size of the coefficients. The effects of ability to pay are particularly precisely

---

10. The coefficient size is an index of the magnitude of the influence of the independent variable (e.g., SAT) on the dependent variable (e.g., institutionally awarded grants), but it cannot be read directly as an estimate of the dollar impact of the change in the independent variable, as it can be in a standard multiple regression. The reason, in brief, is that the Tobit estimate is nonlinear, taking into account the "piling up" of observations at 0. The easiest way to get a feel for the magnitude of the effects of changes in the independent variable is to look at predicted or simulated effects of changes in the independent variables, as we do in the next section of the essay.

estimated. The estimates in Table 4 thus confirm the evidence we presented in our cross-tabulations above: Aid awards in both public and private higher education are responsive to both "need" and "merit."

Recall that the difference between all grants and institutionally awarded grants is that the latter omits Pell and state grant awards to individual students. Since Pell is strongly need sensitive and many state grant programs are need sensitive as well, it is not surprising that the coefficient on need in the "all grant" equations is consistently higher in absolute value than that for institutionally awarded grants, while the reverse is true of the coefficient on SAT. This relationship holds for both public and private institutions.

It is of particular interest to note changes in these coefficients over time. In particular, in private higher education, the coefficient on EFC is statistically significantly lower in absolute value in 1999–2000 than it was in 1992–1993 for both "all grants" and "institutionally awarded grants." That is, controlling for other factors, grant awards varied less strongly with ability to pay in private higher education at the end of the 1990s than earlier. This finding is consistent with the trend we noted earlier in the descriptive tables—that grant awards in private higher education varied less strongly with income in 1999–2000 than in 1992–1993. The coefficients on SAT, on the other hand, are slightly larger in 1999–2000 than in 1992–1993, but the difference is not statistically significant.

In general in public higher education, grant awards are less strongly associated with EFC than is true in private higher education. This may be partly a statistical artifact resulting from lower tuition in public than in private higher education. This lower tuition means that the range of values of EFC across which families qualify for need-based aid is smaller in public higher education—families "top out" of the aid system at lower levels of income. This restricted range may lead to a downward bias in estimating the impact of EFC on grant aid. In public higher education, awards varied slightly more strongly with EFC in 1999–2000 than in 1992–1993, a difference that is statistically significant but not very large. On the other hand, in public higher education, the relationship between grant award and SAT level became substantially stronger from the early 1990s to the end of the decade. In fact, for the case of institutionally awarded grant aid, the responsiveness of grant awards to differences in SAT levels more than doubled (from 3.15 to 6.48). By 1999–2000, the responsiveness of institutional grant awards to SAT was nearly as large in public as in private higher education.

The coefficients we have reported here confirm the major inferences we drew from the simple cross-tabulations presented above, with the important advantage that they include controls for a number of other variables that influence the relationships seen in the "raw data" of the cross-tabs. To assist further in interpreting the findings implicit in the Tobit equations we have just reviewed, we turn to a simulation exercise that allows us to draw out implications of our estimates more explicitly.

Predicted Values

With the help of the equations we have estimated, we can actually "predict" the amount of grant aid of a particular kind a student with specified characteristics attending a given type of institution with a given tuition would be expected to receive. Thus for example, a white man with an SAT of 900 and an EFC at the midpoint of the top quartile of private institution EFCs who attended a private research I university with average tuition in 1992–1993 would be expected to receive an institutional grant of $112. If we vary the value of SAT and of EFC while holding these other characteristics constant, we can present a picture of how private institutional grant awards varied with SAT and EFC in 1992–1993, holding other factors constant. We can perform a similar analysis for all grants instead of institutional grants, for 1999–2000 as well as for 1992–1993 and for public as well as private institutions. The results are shown in Table 9. (Similar analyses could be prepared for black students, for women, or for other institution types, but the predicted results [in terms of the relationships between SAT, EFC, and grant awards] would look similar). Although some details differ, Table 9 can be viewed as an analogue to Table 1, with extraneous sources of variation removed.

The interpretation of this table might be better understood by comparing results for institutionally awarded grants in 1992–1993 at private institutions as reported in Table 9 with those in Table 1. In both tables, we see that grant awards fall as EFC (our measure of ability to pay) rises. The rate of change is considerably higher, however, in Table 9 than in Table 1—going from high to low EFC in Table 9 the change is from $112 to $2,711 dollars, while in Table 1 the change is from $253 to $1,645. Why the difference? Several factors may be at work, but an important one is that, on average, higher-income (lower EFC) students attend more expensive institutions and higher tuition is associated with higher aid. Thus the raw data in Table 1 confound the direct relationship of grant level and EFC with the relationship between grant level and tuition, a factor that comes into play because EFC is correlated with tuition level. Thus, in Table 9 we are able to illustrate our estimates of the relationships we focus on free of these confounding effects.

The table is organized as follows. All continuous variables other than SAT and EFC are assigned their mean values and a predicted value is estimated based on

Table 9. Predicted values of institutionally awarded grants and of all grants in public and private colleges and universities, 1992–1993 and 1999–2000, in 1999–2000 dollars

		Institutionally awarded grants (includes SEOG)			
		Private Colleges and Universities			
		EFC Quartile			
	SAT	High	Upper Middle	Middle	Low
	900	112	1158	1958	2711
1992–1993	1100	226	1824	2891	3835
	1300	426	2717	4057	5184
	900	923	2372	3286	3978
1999–2000	1100	1352	3183	4271	5071
	1300	1912	4150	5404	6305
		Public Colleges and Universities			
		EFC Quartile			
	SAT	High	Upper Middle	Middle	Low
	900	93	243	314	371
1992–1993	1100	152	372	471	549
	1300	243	550	683	784
	900	72	194	284	365
1999–2000	1100	149	362	509	635
	1300	287	631	853	1036
		All grants			
		Private Colleges and Universities			
		EFC Quartile			
	SAT	High	Upper Middle	Middle	Low
	900	151	1739	2927	4013
1992–1993	1100	264	2436	3879	5137
	1300	441	3294	4987	6397
	900	1062	3147	4501	5532
1999–2000	1100	1441	3928	5452	6574
	1300	1913	4813	6497	7709
		Public Colleges and Universities			
		EFC Quartile			
	SAT	High	Upper Middle	Middle	Low
	900	119	581	848	1072
1992–1993	1100	168	746	1064	1323
	1300	232	942	1315	1611
	900	163	678	1114	1510
1999–2000	1100	229	875	1392	1847
	1300	316	1112	1713	2227

those values, the specified SAT level (900, 1100, or 1300) and the midpoint value in the specified EFC quartile. Qualitative variables (race/ethnicity, gender, and Carnegie Classification) are evaluated for the categories white, male, research 1 university.[11] The estimated values reported in Table 9, because they are based on the Tobit analysis presented above, allow for the fact that many observed values in each case will be zero.[12]

These results thus give a picture of the nonlinear relationship between EFC and institutionally awarded grant aid for various values of SAT, and of the nonlinear relationship between SAT and institutionally awarded grant aid for various levels of EFC, evaluated at means for other variables, as estimated by Tobit.

Looking first at the results for private institutions, it is easy to see the positive estimated relationship between SAT and award levels, and the negative relationship between EFC and award levels for both "all grants" and for "institutional grants." This table also allows us to assess quantitatively how grant awards vary with SAT and EFC, and to note the interactions between the effects. Thus, for example, in 1992–1993 the difference in institutionally awarded aid to a high-income (high-EFC) student with a low SAT (900) and a high SAT (1300) was just over $300 in the freshman year; by 1999–2000, the difference was almost $1,000. (Recall that this is after controlling for differences in tuition levels between the institutions typically attended by higher and lower SAT students.) For a low-income (low-EFC) student, the difference in institutional grant aid between having a low SAT and a high SAT in 1992–1993 was larger than that for a high-EFC student (at more than $1,400 for the freshman year), but that difference did not grow in real terms and in fact fell a little (to under $1,400 as we estimate it) over the time period.

Reviewing the temporal comparison more generally for private institutions, it is clear that private higher-education award levels went up substantially for all groups, in estimates controlling for other factors. Interestingly, for low-, middle-, and upper-middle-EFC levels, the amount of increase in award levels (both all and institutional) is roughly constant across both SAT and EFC levels. For high-EFC students (those with the greatest ability to pay), however, changes in award levels are more sensitive to SAT. In fact, for institutional grants, low SAT, high-income students got the smallest increment in dollars from 1992–1993 to

---

11. Substituting other values instead of the omitted variable does not qualitatively change the results.

12. The estimate can be interpreted as a weighted average of the estimated number of 0's and of the mean of the estimated positive values. It should be noted that the standard errors around these point estimates are relatively large. This exercise is the equivalent of predicting the aid award of an individual student, and obviously much of the variation in individual awards is unexplained. It is not the individual point estimates but the relationship among the numbers in different cells that is of interest here.

1999–2000 of any group, while high SAT, high-income students got the largest increase. For this high-EFC group, then, merit seems to be playing an increasing role in aid awards, while for other income groups, merit is not playing an increasing role at private institutions.

We see in Table 9 that in public as in private institutions, grant awards are sensitive to both SAT and EFC. In quantitative terms, the differences in grant awards with variation in EFC and SAT are smaller in public than in private higher education, as would be expected in light of the higher tuitions in private institutions. Still, the differences are not tiny in publics, with for example the institutionally awarded grant aid to a low-EFC, high SAT student during his or her freshman year predicted to be more than $400 greater than that for a low SAT student from the same EFC group in 1992–1993, and nearly $700 greater (after inflation adjustment) in 1999–2000.

In general, there has been an increase in the EFC sensitivity of grant aid in public higher education from 1992–1993 to 1999–2000. This trend is present in institutionally awarded aid, but is much stronger in the "all grants" calculation. The most important reason for this difference is the significant growth in Pell Grants, which are strongly targeted to low-income families, during the latter part of the 1990s. At the same time, the greater estimated influence of SAT on institutional grants for students at all EFC levels comes through in these data. Indeed, low SAT students at all EFC levels had actual reductions in their estimated institutional grant award levels after allowing for inflation. Students at high SAT levels were estimated to have gains in institutional awards no matter their EFC levels, with the highest gains being observed for the low-income group. These results, while stronger for institutional grant awards, are also observed in the estimated results for all grants as well. Thus in public higher education, EFC and SAT both came to have a stronger influence on determining grant award levels during the 1990s.

Stepping back from these time trends, it is clear that at all EFC levels and in both years, private school students with higher SAT scores are predicted to receive larger institutionally based grant awards. For example, for the modestly affluent students in the upper-middle EFC quartile, the predicted difference in annual award level between a student with a SAT score of 1100 and one with 1300 was $893 in 1992–1993 (in 1999–2000 dollars) and was $967 in 1999–2000—a substantial premium in each year. Notice also that, even after controlling for tuition differences, the rewards for higher SAT scores are quite substantial for the lowest income students as well, with a 200-point increase (whether from 900 to 1100 or from 1100 to 1300), leading to award differences of more than $1,000 per year in both years.

In public higher education, award levels are of course generally much lower, reflecting the much lower tuition levels in public institutions than in private colleges and universities. Yet the increase in award levels accompanying higher SAT scores has generally grown in inflation-adjusted-dollar terms, with the largest gains for low-EFC students. The difference in institutionally awarded aid at public colleges and universities for low-EFC students with SAT scores of 1100 and 1300 grew from $235 in 1992–1993 to $401 in 1999–2000 (after adjusting for inflation).

Conclusions

The relationship among financial need, academic merit, and financial aid grants has changed in complicated ways over the period from 1992–1993 to 1999–2000, and the patterns of change are different in private and in public higher education.

In private higher education, two changes are notable. First, there has been a general "flattening" of the relationship between ability to pay and grant award levels. We saw this in the initial cross-tabulations, in the coefficients of the Tobit equation, and in the tables reporting estimated values from the Tobit equation. It's not at all clear that, for the most part, this change should be labeled an increase in "merit aid." For most income groups, we did not discern a clear relationship between the size of the aid increment and the SAT level. It may be most sensible to view this movement of grant dollars toward higher-income (or EFC) families as reflecting not a greater "demand" for high SAT students, but rather an excessive supply of places at many private colleges, leading to a bidding down of the net price.[13] The more neutral term "non-need-based aid" may be more descriptive of this situation than "merit aid," although simply calling this phenomenon "discounting" may make the most sense.

As we noted earlier, net prices have actually fallen (after inflation adjustment) at private institutions for some SAT-income groups, and have risen slowly for others. Competition with lower-priced public institutions coupled with intense competition among private institutions for applicants seems to have retarded increases in net price. Colleges appear to find it effective as a marketing strategy to accomplish this decline (or slowing in the increase) in net price by raising grant awards faster than their increase in sticker price. An alternative practice would be to simply lower the sticker price, but the confusion between price and quality makes that an unlikely practice in all but a few well-publicized cases.

---

13. It is important to bear in mind that at the level of the individual institution, even a student in our low SAT group may be a "merit" student if her or his SAT is above the institutional average. It's possible that there is a merit component in individual award decisions at private institutions that "washes out" at the aggregate level.

The second observation qualifies the first. There is evidence that for the high-income group at private colleges and universities, SAT scores have become more important determinants of grant award levels than earlier. In the cross-tabulations shown in Table 1, there is some indication of this in the fact that the "premium" in terms of institutionally awarded grants to high-income students when SAT scores rise from the middle level to the high level was only $136 in 1992–1993— far lower than for any other income group—but rose to over $1,200 in 1999–2000. However, since the raw data reported in Table 1 reflect the relationships among a number of variables, it is important to use multivariate statistical techniques to see if this pattern is sustained after other variables are controlled for.

And indeed this is what we find. As we see in Table 9, after controlling the SAT–EFC-grant aid relationships for changes in other variables, among low SAT students, the estimated gain in institutional grant aid at privates was smallest for the high-EFC group; among high SAT students, it was the largest. One plausible way in which this result could be brought about is through a combination of "institution-side" and "student-side" factors. More institutions may be turning to merit aid to attract high SAT students, even if those students have a strong ability to pay. It is understandable that they would be reluctant to offer discounts to other students from affluent families who lack strong "merit." At the same time, it is possible that a larger number of affluent students themselves are being encouraged by their parents to accept strong merit offers to save on tuition bills. Our data do not suggest to us a good way to distinguish these possibilities, which may well both be present.

In public higher education, in contrast, there is evidence that institutionally awarded grants have become more sensitive to SAT scores across all income groups—a result we found in the descriptive data, in our Tobit equations, and in the tables showing predicted values of aid in calculations that control for confounding factors. A plausible explanation for this result is that legislators in many states have become more comfortable with the idea of rewarding merit as a legitimate goal for public higher education and more accepting of the proposition that the quality of public higher education in a state can be measured by the qualifications of entering students.

At the same time, we have seen that the net price facing the lowest income students in public colleges and universities fell between 1992–1993 and 1999–2000 and, more generally, that estimated awards rose more rapidly with need (i.e., fell more rapidly with EFC) in 1999–2000 than in 1992–1993. For those who are concerned about access and opportunity this is an encouraging trend. Recent efforts in a number of states to develop programs targeted specifically at attracting highly disadvantaged students suggest that achieving greater opportunity for the economically disadvantaged is seen as both an important institutional commitment and a politically viable strategy.

While not wanting to dismiss these encouraging trends, we should keep in mind that the period we have examined includes an unusually prosperous set of years for public higher education. Following the recession of the early 1990s, a sustained economic expansion filled state coffers and led to large increases in state appropriations in the latter half of the decade, most of which is captured in our data.[14] The federal investment in Pell Grants also expanded substantially during these "boom" years. Since the end of the boom economy in the early part of this decade, the experience of the U.S. economy and of both state and federal governments has been very different. Increases in Pell Grants have slowed substantially, and public college tuitions have risen rapidly without corresponding increases in aid. There appears to be a secular trend toward states devoting a decreasing share of their resources toward public higher education,[15] and it seems to us unlikely that the favorable trend toward lower net prices for low-income students in public higher education has continued into the current decade or will be sustained in the future under current policies.

The findings in this essay add to the growing body of evidence that the principle of awarding financial aid strictly in relation to ability to pay is becoming an increasingly less important factor in the distribution of aid in America's private colleges and universities. For the best endowed and the most selective private colleges and universities, need-blind admissions, full-need funding of admitted students, and minimal use of merit aid remain important and valuable principles. For most other private institutions, such policies are simply unaffordable and the competitive pressures that lead to discounting for affluent students are extremely difficult to resist. Moreover as Bowen, Kurzweil, and Tobin argue, for any given institution, attracting more able students is likely to improve the education the institution can offer to all of its students.[16] Although the pursuit of merit-aid policies for this purpose may be collectively self-defeating, as one institution's gain becomes another's loss,[17] there will

---

14. Michael S. McPherson and Morton Owen Schapiro, "Funding Roller Coaster for Public Higher Education," *Science* 302 (November 14, 2003): 1157.

15. Thomas J. Kane, Peter R. Orszag, and David L. Gunter, *State Fiscal Constraints and Higher Education Spending*, Urban-Brookings Tax Policy Center Discussion, Paper No. 11 (May 2003).

16. William G. Bowen, Martin A. Kurzweil, and Eugene M. Tobin, *Equity and Excellence in American Higher Education* (Charlottesville, Va.: University of Virginia Press, 2005).

17. This will not always be true. To the degree that merit-aid policies result in a net migration of students from more selective institutions (who eschew merit aid) to less selective ones (who do not), there could be net educational benefits from such policies; see McPherson and Schapiro, *The Student Aid Game*.

remain strong pressures to pursue such policies in the absence of enforceable collective agreements. As we have argued elsewhere, there is good reason for government policy to expand opportunities for private colleges to reach agreements on targeting their financial aid resources on needy students without risking antitrust prosecution.[18]

In public higher education, our data suggest that at least in the unusual circumstances of the 1990s, public universities and colleges attempted to become more merit oriented *and* more ability-to-pay oriented at the same time. One might view the ambitious effort by the state of California to incorporate effective means testing as well as merit sensitivity into its Cal Grant program as acting in the same spirit. (This effort has run afoul of California's budget difficulties.) There is a good deal of interest these days in developing programs that would combine the features of being (a) much more understandable and simpler to run than traditional student aid programs; (b) income sensitive, in order to meet equity concerns and keep costs under control; and (c) merit sensitive, for a range of reasons that may include providing incentives to students to work harder in high school, targeting funds where they may have a high payoff, and attracting voters who find allocation by merit an easily justified principle. Our data offer some reason to see public universities as searching in these directions in the 1990s. That said, we know the budgetary circumstances of most states have been poor until recently and that long-run policies are hard to devise and operate in the highly cycle-sensitive environment of state policymaking.

Most colleges and universities in both public and private sectors probably have relatively little discretion to make significant changes in their allocation of financial aid resources on their own. The principal exceptions are the relative handful of exceptionally well-endowed private universities and colleges and the small number of public universities who may have sufficient prestige and market power to set their own policies within limits. To the extent that Americans believe there should be a decidedly different allocation of resources toward higher education and/or a major change in the distribution of financial aid across categories of students, they will need to look to the policies of their state and federal governments to effect change.

---

18. Michael S. McPherson and Morton Owen Schapiro, "Financing Undergraduate Education: Designing National Policies," *National Tax Journal* (Sept. 3, 1997): 557–571.

How Scarce Are
High-Ability, Low-Income Students?

Catharine B. Hill and Gordon C. Winston[1]

Introduction

The growing concern about access to highly selective colleges and universities[2] was heightened by a recently published study of 28 of the most selective private schools in the United States—"the COFHE schools"[3]—that showed that only 10 percent of their students come from the bottom 40 percent of the U.S. family income distribution.[4] While few might have expected that the students at these demanding schools would have been drawn equally from across national family incomes, the 10 percent/40 percent ratio surely demands a better understanding.

1. MiHye Kim got this project underway with her examination of the SAT data and the momentum was continued by Rachel Louis, Ashley Hartman, Carey Aubert, and Jessica England. David Brodigan gave us access to the Williams data. The cooperation of the College Board and ACT in providing data was crucial and is much appreciated. Very helpful comments came from Dave Zimmerman, Robert Klitgaard, Chris Winters, and participants at the Macalester-Spencer Forum in June 2005 and the Forum for the Future of Higher Education at Aspen in September. As usual, the Andrew W. Mellon Foundation's support of the Williams Project on the Economics of Higher Education was critical in making this study possible.

2. William G. Bowen, The Thomas Jefferson Foundation Distinguished Lecture Series, University of Virginia (April 2004): Lecture I "In Pursuit of Excellence," Lecture II "The Quest for Equity: 'Class' (Socioeconomic Status) in American Higher Education," Lecture III "Stand and Prosper! Race and American Higher Education"; William G., Bowen, Martin Kurzweil, and Eugene M. Tobin, *Equity and Excellence in American Higher Education* (Charlottesville, Va.: University of Virginia Press, 2005); Lawrence H. Summers, "Higher Education and the American Dream," speech delivered at the 86th Annual Meeting, American Council on Education, Miami, Florida (February 29, 2004), http://www.president.harvard.edu/speeches/2004/ace.html; Anthony P. Carnevale and Stephen J. Rose, "Socioeconomic Status, Race/Ethnicity, and Selective College Admission," in *America's Untapped Resource: Low-Income Students in Higher Education*, edited by Richard D. Kahlenberg (New York: The Century Foundation, 2004).

3. Including Harvard, Yale, Princeton, Penn, Columbia, Dartmouth, Brown, Cornell, Duke, MIT, Stanford, Northwestern, Chicago, Georgetown, Rochester, Washington University, Rice, Johns Hopkins, Wellesley, Smith, Bryn Mawr, Barnard, Mt. Holyoke, Carleton, Oberlin, Amherst, Pomona, Trinity, Wesleyan, Williams, and Swarthmore. Three of these schools did not participate in the study.

4. Catharine B. Hill, Gordon C. Winston, and Stephanie Boyd, "Affordability: Family Incomes and Net Prices at Highly Selective Private Colleges and Universities," *Journal of Human Resources* 40, No. 4 (Fall 2005): 769–790.

Unfortunately, ideology provides two too-easy answers. One holds that able low-income students who, in all respects, qualify for these schools are excluded by admissions policies designed to protect the children of the wealthy and well-connected from competition—these schools are "bastions of privilege."[5] A quite different ideology holds that more highly qualified students from low-income families would be welcome but they simply don't exist—that everything from inadequate nutrition to tough neighborhoods and weak families and educational systems have conspired to keep many low-income students from being able to pass a perfectly fair cut for admission to these schools.[6]

Fortunately, a third possibility can be ruled out by evidence from that same study of COFHE schools.[7] Most of these schools practice "need-blind admissions with full-need financial aid"[8] with the result that the price actually paid for tuition, room, board, and fees by students from the poorest families (those earning under $24,000 in 2001 in our data) at one of them averaged less than $1,000 a year despite a mean sticker price of $33,831. On average, over all 28 schools, their net price was $7,552, before further adjustments of immediate cost by loans and jobs—less than the average price of a public four-year college.[9] So the *affordability* of these schools is not likely to be an important reason for their meager proportions of low-income students (though students' lack of *knowledge* of these low prices quite likely helps to explain their scarcity.)[10] At these wealthiest schools, it is generally true that a student who can get in, can afford to go.

---

5. Peter Schmidt, "Noted Higher-Education Researcher Urges Admissions Preferences for the Poor," *The Chronicle of Higher Education* (April 16, 2004); Bowen, Kurzweil, and Tobin, *Equity and Excellence in American Higher Education*.

6. Jeffrey A. Owings, Marilyn McMillen, John Burkett, and Bruce Daniel, "Making the Cut: Who Meets Highly Selective College Entrance Criteria?" Statistics in Brief, National Center for Educational Statistics, U.S. Department of Education, Office of Educational Research and Improvement, NCES 95-732 (April 1995); James J. Heckman, "Policies to Foster Human Capital," NBER Working Paper 7288 (1999); Alberto I. Cabrera and Steven La Nasa, "Understanding the College Choice of Disadvantaged Students," *New Directions for Institutional Research* 107 (2000): 5–22.

7. Hill, Winston, and Boyd, "Affordability: Family Incomes and Net Prices at Highly Selective Private Colleges and Universities."

8. So admissions decisions are made without knowledge of family income and the student's price is adjusted so that tuition, loans, and a campus job will make the school affordable to the admitted applicant from even the lowest income family.

9. College Board, *Trends in College Prices* (New York: The College Board, 2004).

10. Susan P. Choy, "Students Whose Parents Did Not Go to College: Postsecondary Access, Persistence, and Attainment," in *Condition of Education 2001* (Washington, D.C.: National Center for Education Statistics, 2002); "There may be substantial costs of simply learning what types of aid are available," p. 95, from Thomas J. Kane, *The Price of Admission: Rethinking How Americans Pay for College* (Washington, D.C.: Brookings Institution Press and New York: Russell Sage Foundation, 1999).

Even without the hyperbole and conspiracy theory of a "bastions of privilege" explanation, though, there remains the possibility that at such schools procedures exist that disadvantage highly able low-income students when they compete for admission with those from wealthier families. So two questions need investigation: Are there, on the one hand, procedural biases that make it harder for low-income students to be admitted to these places and, on the other hand, "Are they out there?" —do many high-ability, low-income students *exist* in the national population? This essay will address the second question while a paper in preparation will explore the first.

"Are they out there?" involves two further questions. What is a reasonable target for the share of low-income, high-ability students in these schools? The 10 percent/40 percent ratio may be worrisome, but what representation would not be? And second, is there a large enough *number* of high-ability high school students from low-income families in the United States for these schools to reach a reasonable target share?

The Target: What Share of These Student Bodies Should Be from Low-Income Families?
The National Population

We take as a reasonable target for these very demanding schools that the income distribution of highly able students in the national population should be mirrored in their student bodies. That, we feel, would embody a meaningful policy of equality of opportunity.[11] If there exists a larger share of low-income, high-ability high school graduates than is found in these schools, low-income students of high ability are underrepresented. Whether that's true, of course, will depend very much on what definition of "high ability" is chosen.

So we examine family income and test score data for the ACT and the SAT over all of the high school seniors who took those tests in 2003. Our assessment of "ability," then, rests on the scores achieved on either of those national tests. We use family income reported by the student test-takers. As measures of ability and family income, these data have shortcomings (discussed more fully in the Addendum), but they have the advantage of large numbers (some 2.3 million test records) and national scope, and they directly address the central question of income and ability.[12]

---

11. The same can be said, of course, for any school with appropriate specification of their student ability levels.

12. What's more, the use of test scores alone to measure student ability gains plausibility from a 1995 NCES study that described a more complex set of five criteria as necessary for admission to a highly selective college and found that a test score was among the most discriminating of single criteria, eliminating 80 percent of the population even when they used an 1100 minimum SAT level (Owings et al., "Making the Cut").

In Table 1, the combined national population of ACT and SAT test-takers is reported by minimum score and by income divided into U.S. census family income quintiles.[13] ACT scores are expressed as SAT equivalents and merged. Under each test score, the first row of the table describes the number of students in the national population who achieved that score *or higher* in each income quintile. The second row under that score shows their distribution (as a percent of those who reported income). So, for instance, the top rows of Table 1 show the number of students nationally scoring 1600 and their percentage distribution across family incomes. The next two rows describe those scoring 1520 or above: 193, or 2.6 percent, of the 7,425 students who scored 1520 or above[14] came from the bottom income quintile; 598, or 8.1 percent, came from the second income quintile; 1,052, or 14.2 percent, from the third; and so on. The next two rows use a minimum score of 1420 to define ability, and so on down to a combined SAT of 400 or above, which, of course, includes the whole population of test-takers. This gives a convenient way to represent the income distribution of students in the population as they are defined by different minimal levels of ability.

It is important that the issue embedded in these numbers is different from that of much of the literature that has looked at the share of high school graduates who meet various college admissions criteria. So the NCES study reported, for instance, that of all "college-bound" high school graduates in 1992, only 5.9 percent satisfied all five of the criteria they identified as needed for admission to a highly selective college,[15] and they examined the effect on the number who passed muster of relaxing each of those criteria.

Ours is a different question. We ask: Of those who meet various minimum SAT–ACT criteria—various potential specifications of high ability—how many of them come from families in each of the five income quintiles? Table 1, then, describes the income distribution of high-ability students, variously defined, in the national population while the NCES study describes how many students in the college-going population *are* highly able.[16]

---

13. For details on the census boundaries and extrapolations for quintile medians, see the Appendix to Hill, Winston, and Boyd.

14. See the Addendum for a discussion of nonreporting of incomes.

15. A senior high school cumulative GPA of 3.5; SAT (or ACT equivalent) of 1100; four English courses, three each in math, sciences, and social science, and two in foreign language; positive teacher evaluations; and evidence of engagement in extracurricular activities (Owings et al., "Making the Cut").

16. It is reassuring that when the 1995 NCES study (Owings et al., "Making the Cut") looked only at those who met all five of their criteria for selectivity and grouped them by family income (SES), they reported results that were quite consistent with those in Table 1—10.4 percent of the highest ability students came from families with the lowest SES.

Table 1. Distribution of students over family income by ability level

National SAT and ACT Test-Taking Population Combined (2003)							
SAT Equivalent Score			Family Income				
Income	Lowest	Lower Middle	Middle	Upper Middle	High	Total Reporting Income	No Income Report
Lower Bound	--	$24,001	$41,001	$61,379	$91,701		
Quintile Median	$15,347	$32,416	$50,890	$74,418	$113,689		
1600	7	30	48	112	252	449	506
Percent	1.6%	6.7%	10.7%	24.9%	56.1%	100%	
1520 or above	193	598	1,052	1,871	3,711	7,425	5,116
Percent	2.6%	8.1%	14.2%	25.2%	50.0%	100%	
1420 or above	1,229	3,047	5,363	8,406	15,288	33,333	20,776
Percent	3.7%	9.1%	16.1%	25.2%	45.9%	100%	
1300 or above	5,982	13,977	23,318	32,912	48,747	124,936	70,334
Percent	4.8%	11.2%	18.7%	26.3%	39.0%	100%	
1220 or above	13,360	30,238	47,683	63,113	85,448	239,842	127,219
Percent	5.6%	12.6%	19.9%	26.3%	35.6%	100%	
1110 or above	36,304	72,706	104,950	128,841	152,152	494,953	238,079
Percent	7.3%	14.7%	21.2%	26.0%	30.7%	100%	
1030 or above	62,404	117,124	158,043	184,752	198,566	720,889	329,027
Percent	8.7%	16.2%	21.9%	25.6%	27.5%	100%	
910 or above	122,412	199,916	245,299	266,401	257,655	1,091,683	464,440
Percent	11.2%	18.3%	22.5%	24.4%	23.6%	100%	
830 or above	173,758	256,333	296,051	307,457	283,905	1,317,504	540,701
Percent	13.2%	19.5%	22.5%	23.3%	21.5%	100%	
740 or above	227,465	303,930	330,957	334,082	297,906	1,494,340	599,439
Percent	15.2%	20.3%	22.1%	22.4%	19.9%	100%	
620 or above	270,223	332,459	348,452	345,527	303,641	1,600,302	638,845
Percent	16.9%	20.8%	21.8%	21.6%	19.0%	100%	
500 or above	286,576	341,063	353,194	348,324	305,050	1,634,207	653,726
Percent	17.5%	20.9%	21.6%	21.3%	18.7%	100%	
400 or above	289,061	342,113	353,654	348,653	305,207	1,638,688	655,841
Percent	17.6%	20.9%	21.6%	21.3%	18.6%	100%	

Two tables in the Addendum report ACT and SAT data separately; we base our conclusions on the combined population, but since we have no way to avoid the double counting of those who took both tests, we confirmed our conclusions using the two tests separately. Within each test population, any test-taker appears only once. And, as noted, the Addendum includes a discussion of the shortcomings of these data in addressing the "Are They Out There?" question and the effects of those shortcomings.

Figures 1a–1m picture the information in the rows of Table 1—the national distribution of test-takers over family incomes for those who scored 1600, those

**Figure 1a. The distribution over family income:
Those with an SAT equivalent score of 1600**

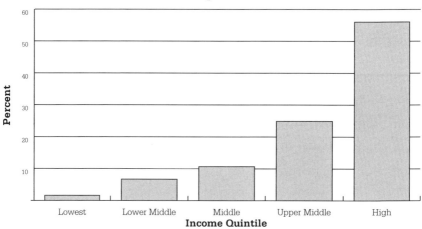

Figure 1b. Those with SAT equivalent scores of 1520 or above

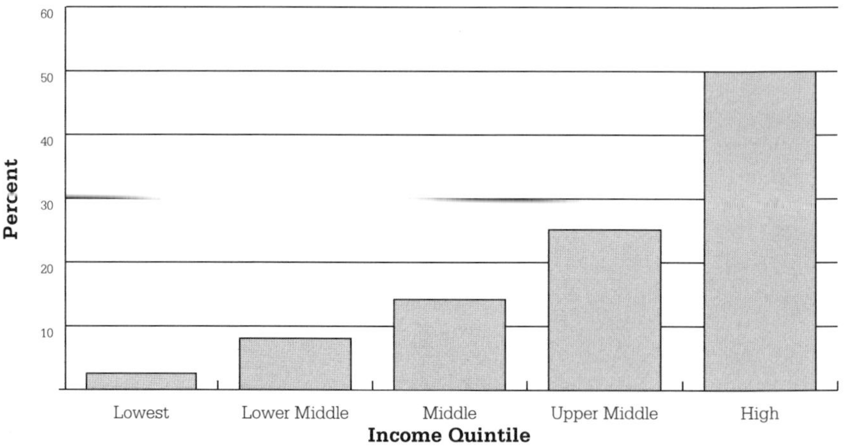

Figure 1c. Those with SAT equivalent scores of 1420 or above

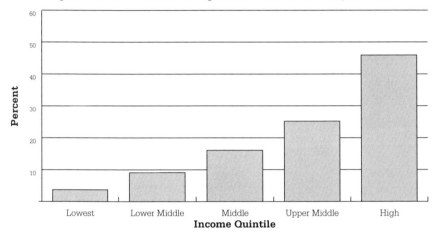

Figure 1d. Those with SAT equivalent scores of 1300 or above

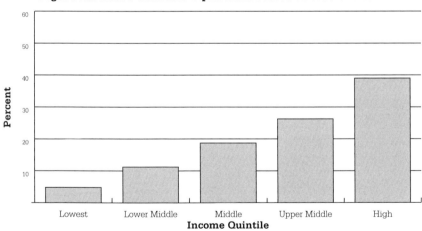

Figure 1e. Those with SAT equivalent scores of 1220 or above

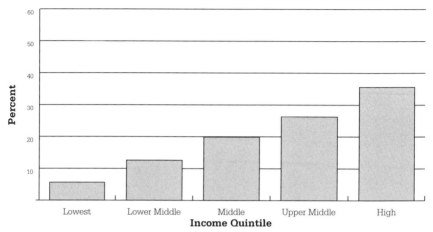

Figure 1f. Those with SAT equivalent scores of 1110 or above

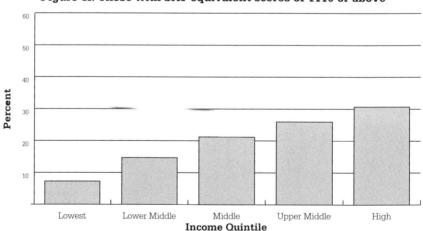

Figure 1g. Those with SAT equivalent scores of 1030 or above

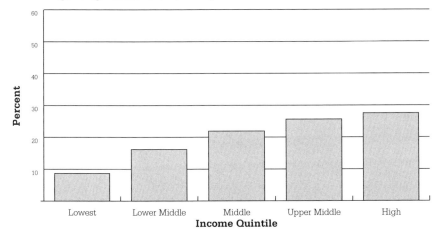

Figure 1h. Those with SAT equivalent scores of 910 or above

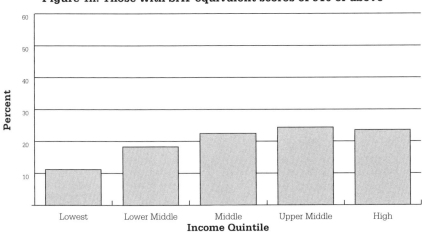

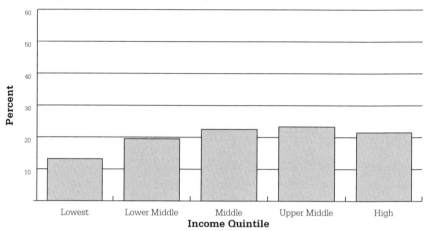

Figure 1i. Those with SAT equivalent scores of 830 or above

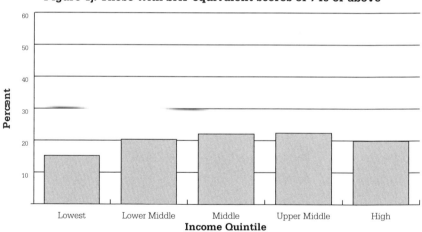

Figure 1j. Those with SAT equivalent scores of 740 or above

Figure 1k. Those with SAT equivalent scores of 620 or above

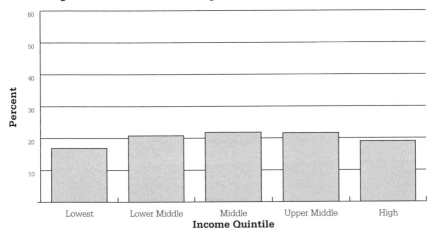

Figure 1l. Those with SAT equivalent scores of 500 or above

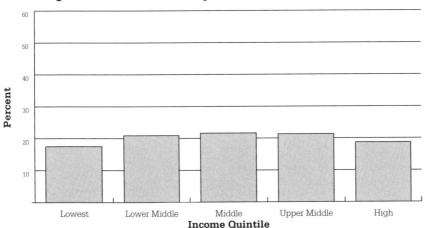

Figure 1m. Those with SAT equivalent scores of 400 or above

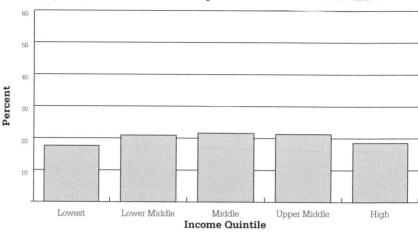

who scored 1520 or above, 1420 or above, and so on down to 400 or above. So, together, these graphs describe the income distribution of that part of the national student population that meets and exceeds alternative definitions of ability.

From the figures, it's clear that with declining minimal test scores the changing shape of the income distributions of the populations they define describes the pattern familiar in national data—as test score minima fall, the corresponding income distribution flattens until, for those scoring 400 or above in Figure 1m (the whole of the population), the distribution is roughly equal across income quintiles.[17] It is clear, too, that the answer to "Are They Out There?" is very sensitive to the choice of a definition of "high ability," so we report alternative measures of high ability.

Low-Income Students in the COFHE Schools

Table 2 is taken from the study of pricing at COFHE schools that triggered the question about whether there are more high-ability, low-income students in the population than are found in these schools. With the same structure as Table 1, it reports the number of students in the COFHE undergraduate population and their percentage distribution over the five income quintiles. With 5 percent from the first quintile (under $24,000) and 5 percent from the second ($24,001 to $41,000), we get the fact we started with: that 10 percent of these students come from the bottom 40 percent of the U.S. family income distribution.

---

17. We would not expect it to be equal across the national quintiles because the population of test-takers is not representative of the national family population.

Table 2. Distribution of students over family income in 28 highly selective private schools (2001–2002)

Income	Family Income					Total Enrollment
	Lowest	Lower Middle	Middle	Upper Middle	High	
Lower Bound	-	$24,001	$41,001	$61,379	$91,701	
Quintile Median	$15,347	$32,416	$50,890	$74,418	$113,689	
Number of Students						
COFHE Schools	5,086	5,956	8,053	12,086	75,803	108,721
Coed Colleges	698	958	1,242	1,951	10,501	15,471
Women's Colleges	532	641	752	962	5,515	8,620
Ivy League Universities	2,079	2,290	3,130	4,747	32,870	45,609
Non-Ivy League Universities	1,777	2,067	2,929	4,426	26,918	39,022
Percent of Total Enrollment						
COFHE Schools	5%	5%	7%	11%	70%	100%
Coed Colleges	5%	6%	8%	13%	68%	100%
Women's Colleges	6%	7%	9%	11%	64%	100%
Ivy League Universities	5%	5%	7%	10%	72%	100%
Non-Ivy League Universities	5%	5%	8%	11%	69%	100%

Comparing the data in Tables 2 and 1, we can see what the COFHE schools would have to do to mirror the income distribution of the national population of high-ability students. Defining high ability with the rather ambitious specification of minimum ability at or above an SAT score of 1420, for instance, Table 1 indicates that 12.8 percent of those scoring that high or higher in the national population come from families in the bottom two income quintiles. The COFHE schools, then, could increase their share of these low-income students by nearly 30 percent while maintaining that very high 1420 minimum standard of ability. If a score of 1300 or above were considered adequate, 16 percent of those who qualify would need to come from the bottom two quintiles—an increase in share of more than half. (The NCES ability cutoff of 1100[18] would see more than 21 percent from low-income families and Carnevale and Rose's definition of high ability as 900 minimum score[19] would have about 30 percent of the COFHE students from the poorest 40 percent of the families.)

---

18. Owings et al., "Making the Cut."

19. Carnevale and Rose, "Socioeconomic Status, Race/Ethnicity, and Selective College Admission."

The lower the ability threshold, predictably, the larger the share of students who would come from the bottom two quintiles. So what are reasonable targets for these highly selective schools? Some data provide a good sense of an answer with information on the interquartile range of their test scores. In the average COFHE school, 25 percent of their students score under 1353 and 25 percent score over 1546. The lowest school score at the 25th percentile is 1160 and the highest is 1400. At the other end, the lowest 75th percentile score is 1375 and the highest is 1580. So it seems reasonable to focus on the income distributions of the six populations in Table 1 that correspond to ability levels defined by minimal scores from 1110 to 1600.

A more complex picture comes from Figures 2a–2f, where the national information on income distribution by minimum scores—the bars from Figure 1—are repeated and contrasted to a similarly defined picture of the income distribution at the COFHE schools. We have little information on test scores for the COFHE students— only their interquartile range and distribution over incomes in the aggregate—so from one panel to the next, the bars describing the schools' populations are the same. In each panel, the COFHE distribution is compared to that of a national population defined by alternative levels of ability, from 1110 to 1600.

It's apparent from the first few figures that the COFHE schools, collectively, do very well by the lowest income, highest ability students. Of those from the bottom quintile who score 1600, a larger share is found in the COFHE schools than the share in the national population.[20] Moving from the first to the second

Figure 2a. Those with an SAT equivalent score of 1600

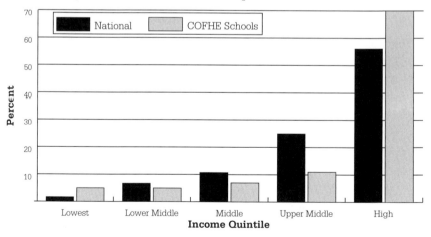

20. This, of course, is consistent with the evidence from Caroline Hoxby, "How the Changing Market Structure of U.S. Higher Education Explains College Tuition," NBER Working Paper 6323 (1997); and R. H. Frank, "Higher Education: The Ultimate Winner-Take-All Market? in *Forum Futures: Exploring the Future of Higher Education, 2000 Papers*, edited by M. E. Devlin and Joel W. Meyerson (San Francisco, CA: Jossey-Bass, 2001), 3–12.

Figure 2b. Those with SAT equivalent scores of 1520 or above

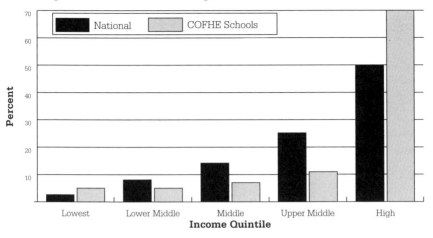

Figure 2c. Those with SAT equivalent scores of 1420 or above

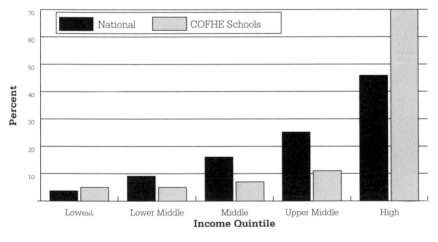

income quintile of students scoring that high, however, COFHE's relative share of low-income students drops, and within the rest of the distribution (the top 60 percent), it is the middle- and upper-middle-income students who are markedly underrepresented, while those from the highest income families are overrepresented at these schools.

As the measure of high ability is moved down the SAT scale in Figures 2b and beyond, the underrepresentation of middle-income students comes to include

Figure 2d. Those with SAT equivalent scores of 1300 or above

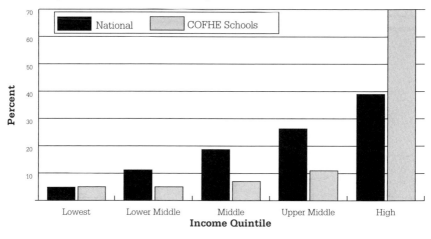

Figure 2e. Those with SAT equivalent scores of 1220 or above

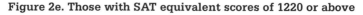

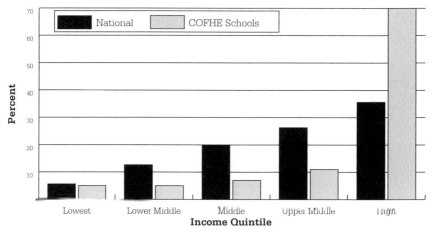

students increasingly from lower-middle-income families and, indeed, even the underrepresentation of students from the bottom two quintiles, relative to the national population, appears to be due primarily to that second quintile—the lowest income students scoring, for instance, 1520 or above, are overrepresented at these schools but not those at higher incomes. Defining high ability with a minimum score of 1420, the lowest incomes are only slightly overrepresented, while the next three quintiles—from $24,000 to $92,000—are underrepresented. For scores 1300 and above, the scarcity of middle-income students becomes more

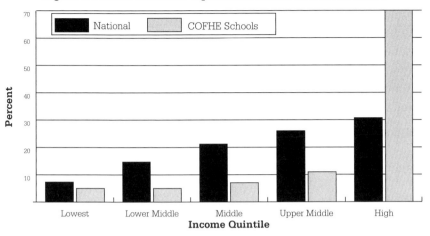

Figure 2f. Those with SAT equivalent scores of 1110 or above

pronounced, and Figure 2d shows that all but the highest income students at that ability level are underrepresented.[21]

The Numbers: Are They Out There?

While the appropriate description of the issue—and the implied policy target—rests on alternative targets that reflect alternative ability levels through which these schools would mirror the population share of high-ability, low-income students, there remains an important question of numbers. We've said, for instance, that if high ability is defined as an SAT score of 1420 or above, the COFHE schools should move, collectively, from having 10 percent to having nearly 13 percent of their students come from the bottom two family income quintiles—they should increase their low-income population by roughly 30 percent. But could they? What does that mean both for them and for the national availability of high-ability, low-income students in the population? If we change the high-ability definition to 1300 or above or to 1220 or above, what does that imply about targets, numbers, and the availability of those students?

A good first cut at "Are the numbers out there?" can be achieved by adding up the figures in the low- and lower-middle-income cells of Table 1 for each specific ability minimum—the supply or availability of such students in the

---

21. These figures, of course, raise the question of whether the target of the COFHE schools should be a representative distribution of income over all income levels or whether there is a special obligation, with a goal of equality of opportunity, to those high-ability students from the lowest income families.

national population– and comparing that sum with the number necessary to achieve the target implied by that ability level, that is, COFHE schools' demand for such students under our suggested policies. So, again, if 1420 were taken as the minimum ability level, the present 10 percent in COFHE schools from the bottom two income quintiles would have to be increased to 12.8 percent— instead of the 2,750 low-income students now matriculating per year,[22] there would be 3,520. That's the schools' demand. On the supply side, Table 1 indicates that at 1420 or above, there are, nationally, 4,276 students in those bottom two income quintiles. So meeting such a target is not impossible, but it's awfully tight: A majority of the low-income, high-ability students in the United States would have to go to one of these COFHE schools in order for them to mirror national population shares under that extreme definition of minimal high ability. If the high-ability definition were reduced to a minimum score of 1300, the enrollment target would become 16 percent, which means that 4,400 would have to be matriculated each year from the low-income population of 19,959 who score 1300 or above. At 1220 or above, the schools' target would be 18.2 percent or 5,005 low-income students per year from a national population of nearly 44,000. As the definition of high ability is relaxed, the target enrollment increases, but not nearly as fast as does the population of low-income students available to meet that target. These facts are summarized in Table 3 for ability levels of 1110 or above to 1600.

So it appears that for reasonable ability levels, these schools underrepresent low-income students and, for those ability levels, the students are, in fact, out there. Some shortcomings with the data, though, make these conclusions a bit too easy.

A large fraction of the test-takers—ranging from 35 percent to over 50 percent in these score ranges—simply don't report family income, so they could not be included in the numbers or percentage distributions of Table 1. Since studies of the distribution of nonreporting over family incomes[23] suggest that low-income students are more likely not to report family income than high-income students, nonreporting most likely leads to understatement of the available population share and number of high-ability, low-income students and of any associated benchmark.

---

22. The schools in our data have a total undergraduate enrollment of approximately 110,000, which implies that 27,500 students are being matriculated each year. With 10 percent of them from the lowest income families, 2,750 low-income students matriculate yearly. A 28 percent increase, then, would see an additional 770 low-income students each year.

23. See the discussion in the Addendum.

Table 3. Availability of low-income, high-ability students to meet yearly enrollment targets

Ability SAT Equivalent Score	Low-Income Target Enrollment: Schools' Demand					Available Numbers: National Supply	
	Target	Low-Income Enrollment Increment Needed to Reach Target			Total Yearly Low-Income Demand		
		Percent of Student Body	Percent of Low-Income Students	Number of Additional Low-Income Students		Q1 + Q2	Maximum Including Non-reports*
1600	8.3%	-1.7%	-17.0%	-468	2,283	37	543
1520 or above	10.7%	0.7%	7.0%	193	2,943	791	5,907
1420 or above	12.8%	2.8%	28.0%	770	3,520	4,276	25,052
1300 or above	16.0%	6.0%	60.0%	1650	4,400	19,959	90,293
1220 or above	18.2%	8.2%	82.0%	2255	5,005	43,598	170,817
1110 or above	22.0%	12.0%	120.0%	3300	6,050	109,010	347,089

The COFHE undergraduate student population is approximately 110,000, of whom 10 percent are from income quintiles 1 and 2 (table above). With 110,000/4=27,500 added each year, 2,750 low-income students each year would represent a steady state.

* If all income nonreports were in the bottom two quintiles.

In the other direction, we know that we double-count those who take both the SAT and the ACT tests, so we know that we overstate the numbers in the data of Table 1 that combines them—and we know that we have no hint of the degree of overstatement. But, like the nonreporting of income, it seems quite likely that high-income students take both tests more frequently than low-income students. While we've tested our conclusions about the distribution of students over incomes by using SAT and ACT data separately,[24] we can't do that to verify our counts of available populations by score. So double-counting of those who took both the ACT and the SAT will have overstated the number of students out there, but that overstatement would appear to affect mostly the high-income students.[25]

---

24. See Tables A1 and A2.

25. Redoing Table 3, underestimating supply by using only those who took the ACT—thereby precluding double counting—would show that there are 2,180 low-income students scoring 1420 or above (against a demand of 3,520), while 11,000 who score 1300 or above are from low-income families (against a demand of 4,400).

Conclusion and Agenda

This paper was motivated by the finding in earlier research that only a small fraction—10 percent—of the students at the nation's leading private colleges and universities come from the bottom two quintiles of the U.S. family income distribution—the bottom 40 percent.[26] The two contending conjectures to explain this meager representation have been that low-income students are being kept out of these schools in order to protect the children of privilege or, alternatively, that a larger share of high-ability, low income students simply doesn't exist in the U.S. population. This paper has looked at the second of these, using national testing data from the SAT and the ACT to find that of those who score well—the highly able students—more than 10 percent do come from these low-income families, but nowhere near 40 percent at any definition of high ability.

There are two implications: These schools can expand their share of low-income students by a nontrivial amount without making concessions in high ability—from 10 to 13 percent even at 1420 or above in these data—so "they *are* out there"; but it is apparent that nowhere near 40 percent are out there. What's happened to low-income students before they reach college age means that few are in a position to take advantage of a highly demanding and selective education, even at a very low price. The easy assumption that anything less than a proportional representation of family incomes at these schools is evidence of exclusion is clearly wrong as even a very generous conception of "high ability"—a minimum combined SAT of 910—finds less than 30 percent of the test-taking population is from the bottom 40 percent of family incomes. It appears that with respect to family incomes, equality of opportunity at these schools can be served; equality of outcome cannot.

The question remains, though, of why the share of low-income students found in these schools is even smaller than their small share in the national population of high-ability students. It provides an extensive research agenda. We do know that these wealthy schools have virtually eliminated financial barriers to the able low-income student through full-need financial aid grants—our earlier study found that the average net price paid by low-income students can be very low, under $1,000 on average for a year at one of these schools.[27] And, recent changes at Harvard and Stanford have further reduced the price for low-income students. (Both schools have eliminated the parents' contribution for families earning up to $40,000 to $45,000, and reduced it significantly for those earning up to $60,000. This change in financial aid policy

---

26. Hill, Winston, and Boyd, "Affordability."
27. Ibid.

also clarifies the message, reducing confusion over exactly what it costs a low income family to send someone to these schools.) But we know very little about what it is that is discouraging highly able low-income students from applying to the nation's best schools or, if they do apply, what may be happening in the admissions process that keeps them from going. So our further research will consider admissions procedures (like basing student search on the population of SAT test-takers rather than on both SAT and ACT, or the effect of increasing reliance on e-mail communication in recruiting, or...). Certainly, the simple lack of knowledge on the part of students about these schools and their opportunities and highly affordable prices, discourages some, and some—even with full knowledge—undoubtedly just won't find them appealing. But if the objective is to assure equality of opportunity—access—for highly able low-income students, we need to know what they're running into—aside from their own personal preferences—that keeps many of them out of Harvard and Stanford and Williams.

Addendum

𝍫 𝍫 𝍫 𝍫

The Quality of the Data

We rely on test scores and students' self-reported incomes to measure ability and family incomes. There are good reasons to be uncomfortable with these and to hope that both the sheer size of the population and the direction of potential distortions give us persuasive results. So it becomes important that these data are being used to describe the share of high-ability, low-income students in the national test-taking population and compare that with their share in the student bodies of this set of highly selective private colleges and universities. As noted previously, since we conclude that a larger share of the high-ability students comes from low-income families in the U.S. population than in the COFHE schools, data problems will weaken that conclusion only if they might lead to *overstatement* of the population share of those high-ability, low-income students.

Student Ability Data

That said, ideally we would judge student ability on the kind of information available to colleges in making their admissions decisions—GPA, class rank, high school courses, extracurricular activities, test scores, etc.,—across all test-takers.

The 1995 NCES study[28] used NELS data to approximate that. Instead, we rely solely on reported test scores, giving a thin measure of ability, but in a very large national database (more than two million test-takers) that also reports variables including each individual's race, gender and, especially usefully, geographic location. Since the issue in this essay is ability relative to family income, the imperfections in our test-score data that raise legitimate worries are those due to (a) multiple test-taking, which has been shown to raise scores, and (b) test-preparation courses that do the same thing. For our purposes, then, it is reassuring that while both of these appear to be income sensitive,[29] raising the relative test scores of high-income students, they therefore tend to *understate* the share of low-income students in the population who would, with the same advantages, show high ability. So a measure of "true" ability (unaffected by repetitive testing or test preparation) would show a larger, not a smaller, share of high-ability, low-income students in the test-taking population.

A different problem is introduced by our combining the populations of ACT and SAT test-takers: Double-counting is eliminated within each test, but we have no way of knowing how many or which students in our data are counted twice because they've taken both tests. While individual admissions departments can and do scan their search data to identify such duplication, we have no way to do that. Therefore, while we've reported the results for the combined populations—expressing ACT scores in SAT equivalents and adding the populations together—we have confirmed all important findings by running the two data sets separately.

Family Income Data

The use of students' self-reported family incomes raises questions of accuracy on the one hand, and of the effect of a large number of nonreporting students on the other. More than 50 percent of those scoring an SAT equivalent of 1600 on ACT and SAT combined don't report family income at all. Lower scores showed a smaller incidence of nonreporting.

The Accuracy of Reported Incomes

Inaccurate income reporting per se would simply add noise to the analysis, but if high- or low-income students report inaccurately in different ways or different degrees, our descriptions of high-ability income distribution might be affected. As noted, however, only if lower-income students were more prone to understate family incomes, would their share in the high-ability population be overstated in our data.

---

28. Owings et al., "Making the Cut."

29. Jacob L. Vigdor and Charles T. Clotfelter, "Retaking the SAT," *The Journal of Human Resources* 38, No. 1 (2003): 1–33.

There is clear recognition in the literature that self-reported incomes can be unreliable,[30] but there is consensus on neither methodology of judging their accuracy nor the shape of any inaccuracies. Studies variously compare family income reports by high school students[31] or community college or public university freshmen[32] or adults[33] with federal income tax returns[34] or parental income reports.[35] Most conclusions are based on comparisons within families but one rests on aggregated state data.[36] There is little agreement on how to measure "accuracy," with some studies appearing to generate their conclusions from their methodology.[37] Finally, some studies consider a number of possible influences on accuracy, including age, gender, education, and family socioeconomic status, and some embed the issue of income accuracy in the question of a broader socioeconomic index. Some studies suggest regression to the mean, concluding that low-income subjects tend to report too much income and high-income subjects too little;[38] some report general overstatement of income;[39] and some report greater accuracy by low-income students.[40]

30. Patrick T. Terenzini, Alberto F. Cabrera, and Elena Bernal, *Swimming Against the Tide: the Poor in American Higher Education*, College Board Research Report No. 2001-01 (New York: The College Board, 2001).

31. Brian D. Kayser and Gene G. Summers, "The Adequacy of Student Reports of Parental SES Characteristics," *Sociological Methods and Research* 1, No. 3 (1973): 303–315.

32. Richard Romano and Louis Moreno, *Response Errors in Reports of Parental Income by Community College Freshmen*, Working Paper Series No. 1-94 (Binghamton, N.Y.: Institute for Community College Research, Broome Community College, 1994); Kris M. Smith and Claudia W. McCann, *The Validity of Students' Self-Reported Family Incomes*, Annual Forum Paper (Tallahassee, Fla.: Association of Institutional Research, 1998).

33. Jeffrey C. Moore, Linda L. Stinson, and Edward J. Welniak, Jr., "Income Measurement Error in Surveys: A Review," *Journal of Official Statistics* 16, No. 4 (2000): 331–361.

34. Romano and Moreno, *Response Errors in Reports of Parental Income*; Smith and McCann, *The Validity of Students' Self-Reported Family Incomes*.

35. William B. Fetters, Peter S. Stowe, and Jeffrey A. Owings, *High School and Beyond: A National Longitudinal Study for the 1980s, Quality of Responses of High School Students to Questionnaire Items* (1984) NCES Number: 84216. If you need more information, see the HS and Beyond site nces.ed.gov/pubsearch/pubsinfo.asp?pubid=84216; Kayser and Summers, "The Adequacy of Student Reports of Parental SES Characteristics."

36. David Card and Abigail Payne, "School Finance Reform, the Distribution of School Spending, and the Distribution of Student Test Scores," *Journal of Public Economics* 83, No. 1 (January 2002): 49–82.

37. As in Romano and Moreno's use of eleven $3,000-wide income brackets that led them to conclude that low-income subjects report income more accurately, neglecting the fact that a much larger percentage error was needed to miss a low-income bracket than a high-income one.

38. Smith and McCann, *The Validity of Students' Self-Reported Family Incomes*.

39. Brian D. Kayser and Gene G. Summers, "The Adequacy of Student Reports of Parental SES Characteristics."

40. Romano and Moreno, *Response Errors in Reports of Parental Income*.

Our conclusion is that no clear picture has emerged from earlier studies that would lead us to believe that biases in the family incomes self-reported by SAT and ACT test-takers inflate the apparent share of high-ability students from low-income families in the national population. Williams's data, described below, reinforces that conclusion: They not only allowed us to look at both the accuracy of self-reported income and the incomes of those who don't self-report income but to do it with a population that represents the high-ability students in which we are interested in this study.

Failure to Report Family Income

The literature on income surveys understandably provides only weak reassurance about the incomes of those who don't report income. Our concern, of course, is that systematic bias in nonreporting by income level might be inflating the apparent share of high-ability, low-income students—if most nonreporting is done by high-income students, then the share of high-ability, low-income students in the population would clearly be overstated. Again, the evidence is mixed. Hasseldenz finds (in a mail survey of Kentucky adults) that nonrespondents have lower incomes (by about 20 percent on average) than those who responded.[41] (Kentucky Department of Revenue incomes were used as "truth.") Another study took a more indirect tack, finding that those lacking household and socioeconomic power and trust were less likely to respond to questions about income in a national telephone survey.[42] These are both pretty far away from the high school test-takers whose income estimates we use, but the suggestion is that low-income students are less, not more, likely to report income. Griffin found both regional and urban–rural differences in response rates, but it is hard to know what to do with that in the present context.[43]

The Evidence from Williams's Data

We're lucky to have a highly relevant, albeit small, population with which to examine both questions of the accuracy of students' family income reports and the incomes of those who don't report incomes. We used six years of data from those 1,440 Williams's students who both filled out the *American Freshman*

---

41. Jon S. Hasseldenz, "Determining Validity and Identifying Nonresponse Bias in a Survey Requesting Income Data," *Research in Higher Education* 5, No. 2 (1976): 179–191.

42. Catherine E. Ross and John R. Reynolds, "The Effects of Power, Knowledge, and Trust on Income Disclosure Surveys," *Social Science Quarterly* 77, No. 4 (1996): 899–911.

43. Deborah H. Griffin, "Measuring Survey Nonresponse by Race and Ethnicity" (Washington D.C.: U.S. Census Bureau, 2003). www.census.gov/acs/www/Downloads/Bibliography/asa02%ODG.pdf.

Survey, with its self-reported family income, and subsequently applied for financial aid, thereby providing an IRS Form 1040 (which we take as as close to the truth about family income as we're likely to come). While the fact that all of these were applicants for financial aid might appear to draw only from a low-income population, the considerable cost of going to Williams (currently a sticker price of $38,000) means that the income range was not as truncated as one might expect.[44]

The two relevant facts that emerged from these data were that low-income students are quite accurate in their estimates of family income and that it is they, rather than higher-income students, who are more likely not to report income at all. If these same behaviors are reflected in the incomes that high-ability students report to ACT and SAT, distortions in the self-reported income data aren't inflating our measure of the share of high-ability, low-income students in the national population. We will be more confident, of course, when we've finished our ongoing analysis of a larger number of students but, in the meantime, these results are both directly to the point and reassuring. So while it remains a possibility, there is no convincing empirical evidence that distortions in self-reported income would cast serious doubt on our analysis.

SAT and ACT Results Separately

The following tables report the SAT and ACT data separately.

It's clear that the conclusions of the text remain. Though the ACT data suggest that there are more low-income, high-ability students in the general population than the SAT data suggest, both indicate that there is a higher proportion "out there" than the 10 percent in the COFHE schools. At a minimum score of 1420, for instance, the SAT population shows that 11.2 percent are from the bottom two quintiles, while the ACT population shows 14.8 percent. Only for those scoring 1520 to 1600 on the SAT is the share of those from the bottom two quintiles under COFHE's 10 percent—a very demanding definition of high ability.

Note that those taking the ACT are in general of lower income than those taking the SAT. So of all SAT test-takers, 35.8 percent are in the bottom two quintiles, while among ACT test-takers, 40.8 percent are in those quintiles. Looking at the other end of the distribution, 44.6 percent of those taking the SAT are in the top two income quintiles, while only 36 percent of those taking the ACT are. Put the other way, the ratio of high- to low-income test-takers is 1.25

---

44. Indeed, in our population, a number of students had family incomes above $100,000.

for the SAT and 0.88 for ACT. Restricting attention to those who score 1110 and above gives the same picture: In the SAT population, 19.6 percent are from the low-income quintiles, while 62.5 percent are from the top quintiles; in the ACT population, those shares are 24.3 percent and 51.7 percent, respectively, and the ratios of high- to low-income test-takers at this ability level are 3.2 for the SAT and 2.1 for ACT. Of course, the fact that we can't identify those who took both tests means that among ACT test-takers, those from high-income families may be more likely also to take the SAT.

Table A1. Distribution of students over family income by ability level, national SAT test-taking population only

SAT Equivalent Score							
	Family Income					**Total Reporting Income**	**No Income Report**
Income	**Lowest**	**Lower Middle**	**Middle**	**Upper Middle**	**High**		
Lower Bound	--	$24,001	$41,001	$61,379	$91,701		
Quintile Median	$15,347	$32,416	$50,890	$74,418	$113,689		
1600	0	20	20	70	190	300	460
Percent	0.0%	6.7%	6.7%	23.3%	63.3%	100%	
1520 or above	80	300	360	830	2,290	3,860	3,820
Percent	2.1%	7.8%	9.3%	21.5%	59.3%	100%	
1420 or above	630	1,430	2,310	4,130	9,830	18,330	15,560
Percent	3.4%	7.8%	12.6%	22.5%	53.6%	100%	
1300 or above	2,790	6,050	9,860	15,990	29,210	63,900	50,080
Percent	4.4%	9.5%	15.4%	25.0%	45.7%	100%	
1220 or above	5,950	12,870	19,870	29,930	50,200	118,820	88,590
Percent	5.0%	10.8%	16.7%	25.2%	42.2%	100%	
1110 or above	15,610	29,550	41,770	59,450	85,990	232,370	159,560
Percent	6.7%	12.7%	18.0%	25.6%	37.0%	100%	
1030 or above	26,510	47,660	62,970	85,250	110,290	332,680	217,380
Percent	8.0%	14.3%	18.9%	25.6%	33.2%	100%	
910 or above	51,300	79,690	96,720	121,440	140,010	489,160	297,840
Percent	10.5%	16.3%	19.8%	24.8%	28.6%	100%	
830 or above	71,850	100,580	116,370	139,300	153,060	581,160	339,340
Percent	12.4%	17.3%	20.0%	24.0%	26.3%	100%	
740 or above	92,510	119,080	130,280	151,750	159,960	653,580	370,160
Percent	14.2%	18.2%	19.9%	23.2%	24.5%	100%	
620 or above	110,890	131,080	138,050	157,380	162,860	700,260	390,630
Percent	15.8%	18.7%	19.7%	22.5%	23.3%	100%	
500 or above	119,080	134,920	140,480	158,970	163,620	717,070	397,930
Percent	16.6%	18.8%	19.6%	22.2%	22.8%	100%	
400 or above	120,830	135,580	140,770	159,230	163,740	720,150	399,320
Percent	16.8%	18.8%	19.5%	22.1%	22.7%	100%	

Table A2. The distribution of students over family income by ability level, national ACT test-taking population only

SAT Equivalent Score	Family Income					Total Reporting Income	No Income Report
Income	Lowest	Lower Middle	Middle	Upper Middle	High		
Lower Bound	--	$24,001	$41,001	$61,379	$91,701		
Quintile Median	$15,347	$32,416	$50,890	$74,418	$113,689		
1600	7	10	28	42	62	149	46
Percent	4.7%	6.7%	18.8%	28.2%	41.6%	100%	
1520 or Above	113	298	692	1,041	1,421	3,565	1,296
Percent	3.2%	8.4%	19.4%	29.2%	39.9%	100%	
1420 or Above	599	1,617	3,053	4,276	5,458	15,003	5,216
Percent	4.0%	10.8%	20.3%	28.5%	36.4%	100%	
1300 or Above	3,192	7,927	13,458	16,922	19,537	61,036	20,254
Percent	5.2%	13.0%	22.0%	27.7%	32.0%	100%	
1220 or Above	7,410	17,368	27,813	33,183	35,248	121,022	38,629
Percent	6.1%	14.4%	23.0%	27.4%	29.1%	100%	
1110 or Above	20,694	43,156	63,180	69,391	66,162	262,583	78,519
Percent	7.9%	16.4%	24.1%	26.4%	25.2%	100%	
1030 or Above	35,894	69,464	95,073	99,502	88,276	388,209	111,647
Percent	9.2%	17.9%	24.5%	25.6%	22.7%	100%	
910 or Above	71,112	120,226	148,579	144,961	117,645	602,523	166,600
Percent	11.8%	20.0%	24.7%	24.1%	19.5%	100%	
830 or Above	101,908	155,753	179,681	168,157	130,845	736,344	201,361
Percent	13.8%	21.2%	24.4%	22.8%	17.8%	100%	
740 or Above	134,955	184,850	200,677	182,332	137,946	840,760	229,279
Percent	16.1%	22.0%	23.9%	21.7%	16.4%	100%	
620 or Above	159,333	201,379	210,402	188,147	140,781	900,042	248,215
Percent	17.7%	22.4%	23.4%	20.9%	15.6%	100%	
500 or Above	167,496	206,143	212,714	189,354	141,430	917,137	255,796
Percent	18.3%	22.5%	23.2%	20.6%	15.4%	100%	
400 or Above	168,231	206,533	212,884	189,423	141,467	918,538	256,521
Percent	18.3%	22.5%	23.2%	20.6%	15.4%	100%	

The Challenge of Improving the Representation of Low-Income Students at Flagship Universities:
AccessUVa and the University of Virginia[1]

Jeffrey Tebbs and Sarah Turner

Students from low-income families are dramatically underrepresented at most state flagship universities, including the University of Virginia.[2] In fall 2004, despite the practice of a need-blind admissions policy, less than 5 percent of the students accepting offers to the University of Virginia were from families with incomes less than 200 percent of the poverty line (about $40,000). At the other end of the spectrum, an astonishing 58 percent of the 2003–2004 incoming class reported family incomes in excess of $100,000. Twenty percent of students reported incomes of $200,000 or more, compared with 2.4 percent of households nationwide.[3]

These sobering statistics reflect a complex network of barriers to "elite" education faced by low-income students, including short-term credit constraints, insufficient transparency in the pricing of public higher education (and the availability of financial aid) and, perhaps most important, substantial differences in measured academic performance between students from high- and low-income families. Generating meaningful "access" to elite public education requires that each of these factors is addressed through public policy. While daunting, a failure to complete this Herculean task might substantially erode public support for flagship institutions of higher education that are charged with the duty of providing opportunities for intergenerational advancement.

In this short essay we focus on the recent strategy known as AccessUVa adopted by the University of Virginia to increase the representation of low-income students at the undergraduate level. We begin by reviewing the basic barriers to "access" at the University of Virginia, which also broadly apply to other selective public institutions. We then summarize the parameters and objectives of the

1. We would like to thank George Stovall and Jesse Rothstein for providing data. Many people at the University of Virginia have been generous in finding time to discuss the design and implementation of the AccessUVa program. We would also like to thank Amanda Pallais for helping to prepare figures. The results and conclusions presented in this paper are the responsibility of the authors.

2. D. Ellwood and T. Kane, "Who is Getting a College Education: Family Background and the Growing Gaps in Enrollment," in *Securing the Future* (New York: Russell Sage Foundation, 2000).

3. Mary Beth Marklein, "The Wealth Gap on Campus: Low-Income Students Scarce at Elite Colleges," *USA Today* (September 20, 2004): 1A.

actual AccessUVa initiative. The third section turns to preliminary analysis of the extent to which the first year of the AccessUVa intervention affected applications, admissions, and accepted offers among students from in-state public high schools that have traditionally been underrepresented in the pool of matriculating students. The final section considers how the long-term effects of the intervention may differ from the immediate impact and discusses the lessons that might be applied in other states from the experience at the University of Virginia.

Barriers to "Access" and the University of Virginia

The Problem in General

No consensus exists in the research literature regarding the reasons for the underrepresentation of low-income students at selective institutions of higher education. In all likelihood, the true state of affairs reflects some composition of the prevailing hypotheses, including credit constraints during the traditional college-going years, information constraints, and the persistence of a strong relationship between socioeconomic circumstances and achievement measured in high school. Whatever the answer is in aggregate, it is important to acknowledge that barriers to enrollment at the most selective institutions may differ from those faced by students deciding whether to enroll in any form of postsecondary education.

At the University of Virginia 2004-05, the total cost of attendance for in-state students was estimated at $12,560 for the academic year, of which $5,243 was tuition and fees.[4] With high direct cost-of-living away from home, low-income students may be particularly likely to commute from home to open access four-year institutions or community colleges rather than incurring the full expense of a residential four-year institution such as the University of Virginia. Thus, despite the financial support available to low-income students through the interplay of federal, state, and institutional programs,[5] it is nevertheless possible that a significant set of students would be required to assume substantial debt burdens.

Beyond direct constraints to financing, observers in both local and national markets have suggested that the reluctance of low-income students to enroll in flagship institutions may stem from information constraints. Three dimensions in which low-income students potentially differ from their affluent peers are their knowledge of

---

4. State Council on Higher Education in Virginia, "2004–2005 Virginia Tuition and Fee Brief," http://www.schev.edu/Students/02-03VATuitionFeeBrief4StudentsParents.asp?from=k12.

5. The maximum Pell Grant is $4,050, and dependent undergraduate students are limited in their borrowing from the federal government to $2,625 in the first year and $3,500 in their second year under the Stafford loan program. Still, even before the introduction of AccessUVa, the University of Virginia was able to offer somewhat more generous aid from institutional sources than other public colleges and universities in the state.

the college application process, their expectations of the value of elite education, and their perceptions regarding the extent to which financial aid will reduce the burden of paying for college. However, in designing and evaluating an outreach program known as College Opportunity and Career Help (COACH) in the Boston public schools, economists Thomas Kane and Chris Avery found that low-income students' understanding of the benefits and costs of college did *not* differ systematically from their more affluent peers.[6] A remaining question for Kane and Avery is whether interventions and intensive counseling designed to help students overcome the complexity of the process of applying for college and financial aid would improve outcomes for low-income students.[7] A quite different type of information constraint is associated with perceptions about "fit"; students from low-income families may face greater uncertainty about whether they would enjoy and/or benefit from residential college life if their parents or acquaintances did not complete a four-year degree.[8]

Finally, persistently low family income may also pose *long-term* credit constraints, which thwart access to optimal levels of primary and secondary schooling, as well as other resources that promote collegiate attainment. The deleterious effects of lower-quality schooling take hold early in childhood, leading to persistent gaps in academic achievement as measured by standardized tests.[9] Indeed, the achievement gap between high- and low-income students is particularly marked at the top of the distribution, from which selective institutions tend to draw. Bowen, Kurzweil, and Tobin report that only 7.4 percent of low-income test-takers score 1200 or better on the SAT, versus 21.4 percent of test-takers in the top income quartile.[10] While the divergence in test

6. Thomas Kane and Chris Avery, "Student Perceptions of College Opportunities: The Boston COACH Program," in *College Choices: The Economics of Where to Go, When to Go, and How to Pay for It*, edited by C. Hoxby (Chicago: University of Chicago Press, 2005), 355–393.

7. There is little evidence to suggest that extracurricular interventions targeted on low-income youth are systematically effective in increasing college enrollment. A recent evaluation of the federal Upward Bound program by Mathematica Policy Research found little overall effect of the intervention on college enrollment and, at best, modest effects on the decision to enter a four-year institution (D. Myers, R. Olsen, N. Seftor, J. Young, and C. Tuttle, "The Impacts of Regular Upward Bound: Results from the Third Follow-Up Data Collection," MPR Reference No. 8464-600 [2004], http://www.mathematicampr.com/publications/PDFs/upboundimpact.pdf).

8. Writing in the *Chronicle of Higher Education* ("Flagship Universities Must Pursue Excellence and Access" [April 22, 2005]), E. A. Ayers and N. F. Hurd note: "In many states, however, students and their parents believe that their flagship university is beyond their financial and academic reach. The rhetoric about 'excellence' and 'selectivity' is understood to mean 'exclusivity.' And there is truth to that suspicion. The drive to excellence may be preventing some of our best public institutions from fulfilling their public role."

9. Pedro Carneiro and James Heckman, "Human Capital Policy," NBER Working Paper 9495 (2003), http://www.nber.org/papers/w9495.

10. William G. Bowen, Martin A. Kurzweil, and Eugene Tobin, *Equity and Excellence in American Higher Education* (Charlottesville, Va.: University of Virginia Press, 2005), 80–81.

scores and college enrollment by family income is unquestionably a national phenomenon, the magnitude of test-score gaps, the concentration of poverty, and the resulting effects on the expected representation of low-income students in selective institutions vary by state.[11]

Stratification in the State of Virginia and the Origins of University of Virginia Students

Virginia is highly stratified on measures of income, family education and, in turn, real resources at the community level. Districts in the northern part of the state (known as NoVA) are among the most affluent and highly educated in the country, while counties in the south ("Southside") are rural and poor with sustained poverty perpetuated by the decline of textile manufacturing and tobacco farming. Figure 1 shows the distribution of household income by county across the state, with these data reported in the Small Area Income and Poverty Estimates prepared by the U.S. Census Bureau in 2002. The median household income (of the median county) in Virginia in 2002 was $36,533. The 25th–75th percentiles range from $30,700 to $47,800. Certain segments of the state possess extraordinarily high wealth, with the wealthiest geographic division (Loudon County) featuring estimated median household income of $87,100. Not surprisingly, family income is inversely related to the percentage of children in poverty. In turn, the areas with the highest proportion of children living below the poverty line are Richmond City (32.9 percent; 13,716) and Norfolk City (27.9 percent; 15,272).[12] Still, many of the places with a relatively high incidence of children living below the poverty line are small towns or rural areas.

Family economic circumstances in Virginia are closely linked to student decisions to take the SAT, their performance on this examination, and ultimately their application and matriculation to the University of Virginia. Using graduation data from the Virginia State Board of Education and enrollment data from the University of Virginia Databook maintained by Institutional Assessment and Studies, we calculate the percentage of spring 2004 high school graduates who enrolled at the University of Virginia the following fall 2004 for each city/county

---

11. See Jeffrey Tebbs and Sarah Turner, "College Education for Low-Income Students: A Caution on the Use of Data on Pell Grant Recipients," *Change* 37, No. 4 (July/August 2005: 34–43). A. Pallais and S. Turner, "Opportunities for Low-Income Students at Top Colleges and Universities: Policy Initiatives and the Distribution of Students," mimeo, University of Virginia (2006).

12. Fairfax County—by far the most populous district in the state—has a child poverty rate of 5.2 percent, representing 12,616 children in the 2000 census.

in Virginia (see Figure 2).[13] The simple correlation measure between family income and the attendance measure is 0.34. We find that the median school district sends 1.61 out of every 100 students to the university. Representation at the University of Virginia, however, varied dramatically by county, with a standard deviation of 2.09. The 90th percentile district sent more than three times as many students (per

Figure 1. Distribution of median household income (by county)

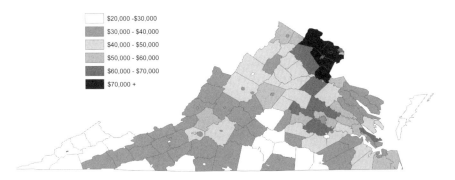

Source: Small Area Income and Poverty Estimates (U.S. Census Bureau, 2002).

Figure 2. Percentage of students graduating from public high schools attending the University of Virginia

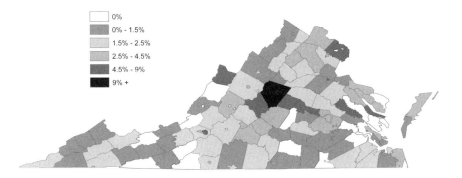

Source: *University of Virginia Databook—IAAS* (Fall 2004), Virginia Department of Education (Spring 2004)

13. Those school districts where high school graduates numbered fewer than 50 are excluded from this analysis.

100) as the median school district, and the highest percentile district sent over 12 out of every 100 graduating students to the University of Virginia. While less than 5 percent of the graduating seniors at most high schools apply to the University of Virginia, there are a small number of high schools where a substantial share of the student body applied to the University of Virginia.[14] As a result, the top quartile of schools in applications accounts for over 65 percent of the applications, while the bottom quartile accounts for less than 2.8 percent of the applications.

Stratification in application and attendance at the University of Virginia is linked to performance in high school as well as family income. Low-income students in Virginia are underrepresented both among test-takers and at the far right tail of the SAT distribution—2.6 percent of test-takers with family incomes less than $40,000 scored better than 1300, whereas over 14 percent of those with incomes over $70,000 scored in excess of 1300. The raw counts are all the more revealing, as we estimate that these percentages represent about 269 relatively low-income students and nearly 2,000 students with family incomes over $70,000. In 2000, students in Virginia reporting annual family incomes of less than $35,000 scored 125 points lower on the SAT than other test-takers.[15] Concurrently, over a moderately high range (1200–1450), low-income students are somewhat less likely to send their scores to the University of Virginia than their high-income peers (see Figure 3).

Although SAT scores are certainly not the only indicator of potential for academic success, the University of Virginia attracts students with relatively high levels of performance as measured by standardized tests. For the cohort matriculating in the fall of 2004, the average combined SAT score was 1330 (659 verbal and 671 math), with 610 defining the threshold for the bottom quartile of students on both parts of the exam. In this regard, students with academic achievement well below this level are not only unlikely to be admitted to the university but might well face substantial academic difficulties if admitted. Thus, the significant test-score gap by economic circumstances in the state of Virginia is a substantial barrier toward increasing the enrollment of low-income students. The score-sending data also reveal that the application stage may also serve as a differential barrier for low-income students.

---

14. Thomas Jefferson High School for Science and Technology (TJHSST), a highly selective magnet program located in Northern Virginia, is a sterling example. Of the 412 students in the 2004-05 senior class, 263 (64 percent) applied to the University of Virginia and 226 were admitted. Less than 1 percent of students at this high school are eligible for free and reduced-price lunches.

15. Tabulations were produced with data provided by Jesse Rothstein and are limited to respondents with known race-ethnicity. For additional details about the data, see David Card and Jesse Rothstein, "Racial Segregation and the Black–White Test Score Gap," mimeo (September 2004).

Figure 3. Percent sending scores to the University of Virginia by score

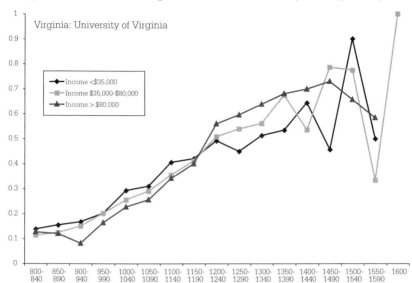

Note: Calculations produced using "test-takers data" covering SAT performance and responses to the Student Descriptive Questionnaire for the year 2000. Data provided by Jesse Rothstein and are limited to respondents with known family income.

AccessUVa Program Parameters

In recent years, mounting concern among administrators at well-endowed colleges and universities has resulted in a flurry of announcements of bold financial aid initiatives. In 2001, Princeton University led the nation by electing to replace student loans with grants. In October 2003, the University of North Carolina announced that all loans would be replaced with grants for students from families earning less than 150 percent of the poverty line.[16] Harvard University has recently implemented a similar (indeed, more generous) program, eliminating financial contributions for students from families earning less than $40,000 per year. Following an overwhelming donation of $100 million for financial aid this past September, Brown University announced that it too would eliminate loans for its neediest students.[17] At the University of Virginia, concern over the impact of the fiscally inevitable tuition increases in 2003 and 2004 on potential students from low- and moderate-income families brought new attention to the adequacy of existing financial aid efforts. At the October 2003 meeting of the Board of Visitors,

---

16. Michael Dobbs, "UNC to Pay Costs of Low-Income Students," *The Washington Post* (October 2, 2003): A13.

17. Greg Winter, "Brown University Receives $100 Million Gift for Financial Aid," *New York Times* (September 15, 2004): 23.

President John Casteen asked staff to craft a plan that would address the impending financing challenges for low- and middle-income students at the university.

To much fanfare, the AccessUVa plan was announced in February 2004. On February 6, 2004, President Casteen announced that starting in fall 2004, the University of Virginia would replace need-based loans with grants for all students below 150 percent of the federal poverty line. Casteen also announced that, starting in fall 2005, the university will cap the total amount of debt any student on financial aid can accrue at 25 percent of the full four-year cost of attendance ($14,520 for in-state students in 2004).[18] All need above that amount will be funded through grants. Additionally, all admitted students will be eligible for one-on-one counseling on "college financing and debt management."[19]

Beyond changes in the availability and distribution of financial aid, the AccessUVa program includes an aggressive outreach and public information campaign designed to "get the word out" that students from all economic circumstances have the opportunity to attend the university. While the financial aid changes are well documented, improvements in recruitment strategies are more challenging to record. These steps include:

- Increases in the number of visits to high schools in relatively low-income areas that have traditionally not sent large numbers of students to the university;

- Public service announcements on radio and in other media touting the openness of the University of Virginia to students with financial need;[20] and

- More aggressive assistance from the financial aid office in helping students to complete FAFSA forms and understand financial aid options.

To illustrate, in fall 2004, the admissions office sent staff to visit an additional 117 high schools in the Virginia area that had not received visits in the prior year. Public

---

18. This cap refers to the full four-year cost for an in-state student, but applies to in-state and out-of-state students alike. The policy thus represents a tremendous boon to low-income students from other states. In light of the far greater magnitude of subsidy provided to out-of-state students, future research ought to include non-Virginia high schools. For the sake of analytic clarity, however, we have limited the data set to students from Virginia.

19. The final modification to AccessUVa was announced in January 2005. Eligibility thresholds for having full demonstrated financial need met exclusively through grants (without loans or work-study) were lifted from 150 percent to 200 percent of the poverty line. Maximum annual family income for full participation in AccessUVa was thus raised from roughly $28,700 to $38,300 for a family of four. See Carlos Santos, "U. Va. Expands Financial Assistance; Students from Families at 200 Percent of the Poverty Level to Qualify," *Richmond Times Dispatch* (January 18, 2005): B1; see also "AccessUVa: How It Works," http://www.virginia.edu/accessuva/how.html.

20. Using the slogan, "Got the Brains but Not the Bucks? The Door Is Open," the advertisements feature actor Sean Patrick Thomas, a University of Virginia alumnus, and encourage general inquiries from potential students.

service announcements were distributed to 16 Virginia television stations, 68 radio stations, and 96 daily and weekly newspapers. In addition, the public service announcements were included in the nationally televised University of Virginia basketball and football events. Mailings, including brochures and posters, were sent to all high schools in Virginia as well as to 9,300 community organizations and churches as part of the effort to disseminate information about the program. Certainly, there is much enthusiasm and determination surrounding the objectives of AccessUVa at the university level, as discussions with staff reveal commitments from many offices. Moreover, aggressive financial aid strengthens the university's hand in negotiations for greater autonomy (including setting tuition), while the need to gain public endorsement for greater autonomy increases the visibility and internal support for policies like AccessUVa.[21] The result is a set of policies coupling higher tuition with higher financial aid in long-term projections.

A Preliminary Look at High-School-Level Effects of AccessUVa

With AccessUVa now in effect for a full application and admissions cycle, it is natural to ask how well the program is working, while at the same time reserving judgment about its potential long-term effectiveness. It will be more than four years before the first cohort of students recruited and admitted under this initiative reaches the expected point of graduation. Moreover, some of the program's most significant impacts may well accrue to those students who are early in their high school careers and are able to adjust their expectations and efforts to the promise of a university education.

While microdata at the level of the individual are not available at each stage in the process (applications, admissions, and matriculation) for the class admitted for the fall of 2005 (as well as prior years), data by high school are available for the public schools in Virginia. For the first-year classes entering in 2002 through 2005, we observe the number of applications, the number of students admitted, and the number of students accepting the offer of admission, in addition to various characteristics about the high school and community that indicate whether the high school serves a disproportionate number of economically

---

21. Sarah Turner ("Higher Tuition, Higher Aid and the Quest to Improve Opportunities for Low-Income Students in Selective, Public Higher Education, in *What Happening to Public Higher Education*, edited by Ronald Ehrenberg [Westport, Conn.: Greenwood Press for the American Council on Education, 2006]) argues that the coincidence of the Restructured Higher Education Act with the introduction of AccessUVa will strengthen the institutional resolve to improving the representation of students from low-income families. While the Restructured Higher Education Act will bring much higher tuition levels, the "coupling" of these efforts will make it much more difficult for the university to abandon or retrench on the "high-aid" strategy if faced with fiscal constraints.

disadvantaged students. These measures include the share of students receiving free or reduced-price lunches and the level of income and education in the surrounding community. We treat these measures as constant over the period of analysis.

Thus, the empirical question we explore is whether the representation of *students from high schools* in Virginia that serve higher proportions of poor students rises with the initiation of the AccessUVa program at the various stages in the matriculation pipeline. We treat observations in the years before the application process that began in fall 2005 as the baseline or "control" and examine the extent to which high-school-level applications, admissions, and acceptances increased at schools serving low-income students after the introduction of AccessUVa. We assume that no other secular changes or policy interventions beyond the program initiation differentially affected those high schools identified as serving low-income students.

The first prong of the AccessUVa policy initiative is to better disseminate information about the financial aid available at the University of Virginia, which should serve to increase overall applications to the university. If the AccessUVa program operates at the margin of altering outcomes for students in schools serving disproportionate numbers of low-income students, we should expect more applications, admissions, and acceptances at these institutions relative to other public high schools in the state.[22]

In short, the number of high school seniors in Virginia has risen over the past several years, and the number of applications has followed suit.[23] However, utilizing regression analysis, Tebbs finds that applications to the university did not rise disproportionately for public high schools with a higher fraction of poor students following the first year of implementation

---

22. Measures of student eligibility for free and reduced-price lunches (FRPL) are from the 2002–2003 Common Core of Data collected by the National Center for Education Statistics (NCES). Application and NCES data are merged with enrollment figures from the Virginia Department of Education. These include the total number of students in the senior class of every Virginia high school from 2002 to 2005.

To qualify for free lunches, students must have a family income less than 130 percent of the poverty line. This equates to approximately $24,900 for a family of four (with two children). To qualify for reduced-price lunches, students must have a family income less than 185 percent of the poverty line, which is equivalent to roughly $35,440. The median high school in the data set has 23.3 percent of students on free or reduced-price lunches. The 25th to the 75th percentile stretches from 14.1 percent to 34.5 percent of eligible students.

23. However, admissions and acceptances from private institutions in the state have not increased between the early years and 2005. To the extent that most of the students at private schools are not low income, we would not expect this to be a margin where the program effects of AccessUVa are most apparent.

of AccessUVa.[24] Comparing outcomes by geographic district (rather than by school) yields parallel results.[25]

Among students from public high schools, admissions and matriculation also rise over the time period.[26] We find a dramatic increase (27.3 percent) between fall 2004 and fall 2005 in the number of students admitted from high schools serving low-income populations, with this change far exceeding the 3 percent increase among the other public schools. The growth (22 percent in the short 2004 to 2005 interval) in admissions from relatively poor districts far outstrips the modest growth seen among students from other public high schools. The acceptances—or planned matriculation—show further differential growth at the schools predominately serving low-income students. The takeaway message is clear: There has been a significant change in the expected representation of students from relatively low-income areas with the advent of AccessUVa, but nearly all of this change has come through the admissions and matriculation margins.

There are two dimensions in which the foregoing analysis is particularly incomplete in providing leverage on the evaluation of AccessUVa. First, more than a quarter of first-year students (and a far higher fraction of applicants) are from states outside of Virginia and, as such, this in-state analysis misses any change in the socioeconomic composition of out-of-state applicants and matriculants. Second, although a student's own family income and average income at a student's high school are likely to be related, they are far from perfectly correlated. An increase in the enrollment of poor students attending high schools in relatively high-income areas would be missed in this high-school-level analysis, while increases in the number of children of highly educated professional parents attending relatively poor schools are highlighted.

A different angle on the recent changes in applications, admissions, and acceptances is provided in data distinguishing income in terms of eligibility for the full (no loan) provisions of AccessUVa at the individual level. These data, for the cohorts entering in fall 2004 and fall 2005 are shown in Table 1 on page 114. Overall, the change in applications is considerably larger than what is apparent in the regression analysis limited to public high schools in Virginia. The continued popularity of the University of Virginia among out-of-state students may contribute to the overall rise, while concerted outreach efforts in the D.C.

---

24. Jeffrey Tebbs, "Redefining 'Access': A Preliminary Evaluation of the University of Virginia's New Financial Aid Initiative," senior thesis, University of Virginia (2005).

25. If there is only one high school in a district (as is the case in many rural counties), these two measures will overlap considerably.

26. Note that, throughout, "acceptances" may well be an upper bound as their appearance or "yield" in the fall has yet to be realized.

Table 1: First-time, first-year admissions data for 2004 and 2005

	Fall 2004			Fall 2005		
	Completed Applications	Offered Admission	Accepted Offer	Completed Applications	Offered Admission	Accepted Offer
Did not apply for financial aid	7,752	2,676	1,461	7,849	2,697	1,424
Applied for financial aid, Income > 200% Poverty Level	6,381	2,818	1,503	7,045	2,889	1,490
Applied for financial aid, Income <200% Poverty Level [AccessUVa eligible]	689	266	133	764	312	200
	Change in Levels (2005 vs. 2004)			Percentage Change (2005 vs. 2004)		
Did not apply for financial aid	97	21	-37	1.3 %	0.8 %	-2.5 %
Applied for financial aid, Income > 200% Poverty Level	664	71	-13	10.4 %	2.5 %	-0.9 %
Applied for financial aid, Income <200% Poverty Level [AccessUVa eligible]	75	46	67	10.9 %	17.3 %	50.4 %

metropolitan area may partially explain the somewhat larger rise in low-income applications apparent in this table. In this presentation of the data, the storyline of interest is related to changes in the "yield." University officials have witnessed a substantial increase in the acceptance of offers of admission by low-income students, with the percentage of those students (first-year, family income less than 200 percent of the poverty line) accepting their offers of admission rising from 50 to 64 percent between fall 2004 and fall 2005. The proverbial "bottom line" from these data is that the representation of low-income students among students accepting admission to the University of Virginia increased markedly between the entering classes in 2004 and 2005—by 39 students or about 30 percent. While such a relative gain appears impressive, the proportion of students meeting the no-loan criteria of AccessUVa with incomes less than 200 percent of the poverty line remains less than 6 percent of the expected cohort for fall 2005.

Conclusions

An early appraisal of the impact of AccessUVa on the participation of low-income students at the University of Virginia suggests that, at least in the short term, greater attention to the circumstances of low-income students in the admissions process combined with efforts to provide information and financial aid have enhanced the willingness of low-income students to accept offers of admission to the university.

Over time, one might suspect that the aggressive outreach efforts, including the public information campaign, will have a significant impact on high school achievement and individual application choices. Ideally, students in the early years of school, if not earlier, will alter their expectations about the affordability of higher education and, in particular, their opportunities at selective institutions like the University of Virginia. Obviously, such gains will require several years to accrue. For now, the modality by which even the most ambitious financial aid programs potentially transform a promise of "access" to a top-tier college into raised expectations (and achievement) remains to be determined. As such, we caution against fixating on any particular approach toward increasing applications and achievement of low-income students. At this stage, administrators and policymakers must instead emphasize experimentation, observation, and analysis in order to correctly identify those strategies that effectively improve student outcomes.

To be sure, the sizable disparities in academic preparation at the secondary level between students from low-income families and affluent families represent the most significant barrier to accessing the advantages of selective higher education. Ultimately, improving the representation of low-income students at selective institutions like the University of Virginia will require that improved financial aid offerings and outreach at the institutional level operate in tandem with substantive reform at the K–12 level.

Six Institutional Perspectives on Socioeconomic Diversity

III

David W. Breneman

Introduction

If asked, "Does your institution support increased educational opportunity, or does it seek to preserve a privileged class?" one can hardly imagine a college or university president responding in any way other than to support opportunity, whether defined by race and ethnicity or by socioeconomic class. Few, if any, presidents would assert that the purpose of their institution is to serve, in the words of Bowen, Kurzweil, and Tobin, as a "bastion of privilege."[1] And yet, one is reminded of the admonition, "Watch what I do, not what I say." Indeed, one of the central messages of the Bowen et al. volume is to note the significant socioeconomic stratification of selective colleges and universities, where students whose parents have not attended college and who come from low-income families are but modestly represented. The conference, Opportunity or Preserving Privilege: The Ambiguous Potential of Higher Education, sponsored by Macalester College and the Andrew W. Mellon Foundation and the Spencer Foundation, was devoted to the issue of enrollment prospects for low-income, first-generation college students throughout our "system" of colleges and universities, selective and nonselective alike. One dimension of that exploration, in addition to the essays in this volume, was to hear directly from presidents or top administrators of six institutions, representing not only highly selective schools but also the broader range of opportunities in both public and private sectors of higher education. This essay summarizes the key points presented by these six panelists, each of whom was asked to comment on the conference theme from the vantage point of a particular institution.

The conference papers, together with the panels of institutional leaders, drove home two points worth noting. First, while federal and state policies regarding student financial aid—and for state universities, tuition levels as well—are important, the ultimate actors of significance in the search for increased socioeconomic diversity are the institutions themselves. Financial aid, regardless of source, is a necessary but not sufficient condition for enrolling more low-income, first-generation college students. A moment's reflection will indicate

---

1. William G. Bowen, Martin A. Kurzweil, and Euguene M. Tobin, *Equity and Excellence in American Higher Education* (Charlottesville: University of Virginia Press, 2005).

that precollegiate circumstances, including high school quality, courses taken, advising, parental support (or lack thereof), and peer influence, together with family income, play critical roles in determining whether (and where) a student applies for college. Although colleges and universities may intervene in modest ways on these precollegiate experiences, for the most part they are beyond the reach of admissions offices and faculty.[2] When the college application process does begin, recruiting efforts, visits to high schools by admissions personnel, quality of student advising by high school faculty and counselors, and peer influence all play central roles, along with the cost of college attendance, in determining where students apply and how their applications are reviewed. Bowen et al. make the case that selective institutions should "put a thumb on the scale" in admitting young people who have overcome the problems associated with low incomes and have managed nonetheless to make it into the admissible pool of candidates, an action that only an admissions office can take. Simply responding to financial need alone, it is argued, will not be sufficient to overcome the academic, social, and cultural barriers that students from low-income backgrounds must surmount, not only to enroll but to succeed in demanding college settings. As a result, institutional policies adopted by college leaders are determinative in this arena—there is nowhere else to look for results.

A second point made clear by the six panelists is the unique situation facing every college and university in this country—unique in terms of history, mission, wealth, location, competition, aspiration, and opportunity set. After listening to the six presentations, one came away with an understanding that each institution will necessarily approach inclusiveness from a distinct vantage point, with differing capabilities to address the issue. One can forecast, therefore, that success (however defined) will vary among institutions, with no cookie-cutter approach applicable. The result is likely to be messy and irregular, defying those who seek order and precision. But such is the inevitable result of our highly decentralized "system" of higher education, one of its strengths but also a source of frustration.

Six Institutional Stories
Private Institutions

The first panel focused on private colleges and universities, represented by Nancy Vickers, president of Bryn Mawr College; Anthony Marx, president of Amherst College; and Henry Bienen, president of Northwestern University.

---

2. Also see the essay in this volume by Patrick Callan et al. for suggestions of ways higher education could link more closely to K–12 schools.

Bryn Mawr College: President Vickers began by giving some basic facts about Bryn Mawr, a residential liberal arts college near Philadelphia with 1,200 undergraduate women students and 400 graduate students, male and female. Her remarks were generally limited to a discussion of the undergraduate student body.

She provided aggregate data on the five remaining women colleges among the original "Seven Sisters": Barnard, Bryn Mawr, Mt. Holyoke, Smith, and Wellesley. She argued that all five have become considerably more diverse in socioeconomic terms in the last 25 years, with over 50 percent of first-year students receiving institutional grant aid. She also noted that about 27 percent of enrollments were students from families with incomes under $50,000, while the median SAT score for the five schools is about 1320, lower by roughly 100 points from a group of peer coeducational colleges. Her point was that these lower SAT scores reflect the reality of having a significant proportion of high-need students in the women's colleges because these students on average achieve lower SAT scores than their more affluent counterparts. The flip side of this observation is the fact that Bryn Mawr has already achieved the goal set by Bowen et al. for enrollments from the bottom-income quartile (the authors had suggested an increase from 11 to 17 percent).

Such gains have not come without their costs, however, for Bryn Mawr does not have endowment resources as large as many of its peers (its endowment is roughly $500 million), which leaves Bryn Mawr more dependent on tuition. Awarding substantial amounts of institutional financial aid reduces net tuition revenue for the college. Thus, while Bryn Mawr is near the top of its peer group in institutional dollars expended for financial aid, it is near the bottom in faculty salaries, a clear tradeoff.

She then focused on two challenges that the college faces in promoting a strong and cohesive educational culture, given its socioeconomic diversity and relatively small size. Since the students tend to know each other on a small campus, differences in income show up clearly in everything from clothes, to cars, to electronics in dorm rooms. To cite but one example, students receiving financial aid often work in dining services, drawing a clear distinction between those full-pay students who become privileged customers, and those who must work to earn their way. Some of the scholarship students interpret this difference in status as demeaning, while others bond with the low-income staff and develop leadership skills from the experience. Nonetheless, class distinctions are there to be seen by all, and can serve to divide the student body into the haves and the have-nots.

The second challenge is budgetary. In the decade from 1993 to 2003, Bryn Mawr's tuition discount rate[3] increased by about 1 percentage point per year,

---

3. A rate determined by dividing the institutional dollars devoted to financial aid by the gross tuition that would have been earned if all students had paid full tuition.

reaching 43 percent in 2003. As tuition is a major source of income, the college is attempting to scale that percentage back, and managed to reduce it to 41 percent in 2005. The ensuing balancing act that is necessary to lower the discount rate while still attracting and helping to finance low-income students is a constant tension that the college faces. (I should note that this issue confronts many private colleges outside the small group with exceptional endowments.[4]) For all but the wealthiest colleges, it serves no purpose to ignore this financial dilemma and strike moral poses; many colleges simply must enroll a reasonable percentage of full-pay students in order to balance the budget.

President Vickers ended her remarks by noting (in agreement with Bowen et al.) that socioeconomic diversity is not a substitute for racial/ethnic diversity; the issue is not one of "either/or" but "both/and." She also argued that it is imperative for colleges to review their admissions criteria as part of this effort, noting that income is an inadequate proxy for socioeconomic status; i.e., the "socio" matters as much as the "economic." One way to sort out that distinction is to consider both income and parental educational background, for a teacher's or a minister's family may be low income, but hardly as disadvantaged culturally as a family with similar income but less formal education. She posed the question, "Is the 1100 SAT student from a low-income, first-generation, college-going family *equal* to the 1300 or 1400 SAT student from a high-income family?" Finally, looking ahead at what we know about future demographics, if colleges continue to increase tuition at current rates while family incomes for those in the bottom-income quartile rise but little, then financing problems will compound. The tradeoffs faced by colleges in this sector seem likely to grow more intense.

Amherst College: In his remarks, President Anthony Marx of Amherst College emphasized values more than data, arguing that schools such as his have a clear obligation to do more than they have been in recruiting and helping to finance enrollment of low-income students. Indeed, he noted that Noah Webster wrote into the college's charter a statement indicating that its mission was to train "indigent young men." Marx observed wryly that the Amherst of today had moved a long way from that objective.

Marx also had harsh remarks for the nation's "system" of financial aid—a combination of federal, state, and institutional funds, requiring complex, complicated, and confusing forms to be filled out, worse than IRS income tax returns. If one way to draw less sophisticated but bright young people into selective colleges is to provide a transparent financing mechanism, the country has clearly

---

4. For a discussion of this issue, see William G. Bowen and David W. Breneman, "Student Aid: Price Discount or Educational Investment?" *Brookings Review* 11 (Winter 1993): 28–31.

failed. Even the price charged adds to the mystery: The tuition price does not cover the real cost but is high enough to antagonize full-fee payers and scare off lower-income prospective students who do not understand or trust financial aid.

Indeed, the admissions system itself can easily appear to low-income prospective students as discriminatory toward them. Early Decision rewards those willing to commit to come before they know the cost of doing so, which low-income students cannot do—and the percentage of students admitted in early decision or early admit plans continues to rise for irresponsible reasons. Admissions often favors those who excel at sports or other extracurricular activities that low-income students have never heard of, did not have access to, or cannot join given the need to work to supplement family income. The SAT is heavily weighted though it may be biased against the poor, especially because they cannot afford coaching or multiple attempts at the test.

He also had harsh words for the higher education community that has failed to do more to ensure vibrant and excellent K–12 schooling. He noted, as have many others, that higher education acts as if it has no responsibility for its feeder K–12 system, somehow expecting it to produce talented and well-prepared students for college, while doing little to help make that happen.

Finally, he argued that the *U.S. News & World Report* rankings of college quality could be designed to reward campuses that do more to include low-income students by including measures of campus diversity and institutional financial aid in its ratings. As it now stands, the ranking procedures may actually do the reverse, as measures of selectivity play heavily into higher scores, though the focus on selectivity may work against an emphasis on identifying and attracting a more diverse student body.

Marx ended his comments by referring to an issue that concerns many in the private sector. Amherst is one of a small number of private colleges and universities with substantial endowment wealth per student and high selectivity. Colleges situated in that favored position have the resources to undertake much more aggressive forms of aid than at present, and in recent years Princeton and Harvard, to name but two, have announced policies of essentially full-grant support for admitted students from families below certain income levels. Each of these policies when announced sent a shock wave through the system, as competing institutions that are not as wealthy cannot afford to implement similar plans. The upshot, Marx worries, may be even greater socioeconomic stratification of higher education overall if the handful of extremely wealthy schools sets policies that close rivals cannot match. This was an issue not resolved in the panel discussion, but to which various members of the audience returned throughout the two days of discussions.

Northwestern University: President Henry Bienen immediately sought to distinguish the economics of his institution, a research university, from the economics of private liberal arts colleges, such as Bryn Mawr and Amherst. The driving force at Northwestern is the need to finance and maintain a research infrastructure of laboratories and related facilities, as well as the research faculty and staff required to be competitive for grants, high quality graduate students, and additional top faculty. He indicated that when he came to Northwestern a decade ago his charge from the trustees was to significantly enhance Northwestern's capacity and standing within the world of research universities, and such spending simply takes priority over expenditures to further diversify the undergraduate student body. In the latter regard, he argued that Northwestern has devoted substantial funds for need-based financial aid for undergraduates (its discount rate is 25 percent) and, with only a few exceptions (athletics and music), the university has not followed a policy of awarding merit aid. Unlike several highly selective institutions, Northwestern has not opted to eliminate all loans from the financial aid packages of students with extreme financial need; indeed, Bienen argues that it is sound policy for all students on aid to incur some debt for their educations. (The average indebtedness of Northwestern graduates is about $16,000, against total charges over four years of nearly $175,000, a ratio of 9 percent that he believes to be both reasonable and manageable.) He further noted that recently Northwestern has experienced the greatest difficulty in enrolling students from families with incomes in the $50,000 to $75,000 range, enrolling 24 percent of all grant recipients in that income group in 2000 versus only 15 percent in 2004.[5]

Another factor that differentiates Northwestern from the smaller colleges is that the university admits students directly to six separate schools, with distinct admissions criteria for each school. Federal and state student aid both play smaller roles today at Northwestern than was true a decade ago, leaving the institution more reliant on its own sources of funds for financial aid. Given the competing priorities of its research emphasis, however, Bienen was very clear that the university would not be able to expand the share of its total budget devoted to undergraduate financial aid.

Discussion: At the close of the three panel presentations, moderator Neil Grabois of Carnegie Corporation noted three issues that he thought were of paramount importance:

---

5. One should note, however, that in 2000, 37 percent of all grant recipients came from families with less than $50,000 income, while in 2004 that number dropped to 22 percent. Northwestern is clearly enrolling fewer grant recipients in all income groups below $75,000 now than four years ago.

1. The clear need to balance competing values and conflicting priorities for expenditure, given the limited resources that even these relatively wealthy institutions possess;

2. The differences in policy and values toward student debt that had been expressed, ranging from no loans to low-income students to reasonable and expected levels of debt; and

3. The worrisome impact that the wealthiest institutions have on the rest of the private sector, as they set policies that others cannot match.

In the general discussion that followed, William Bowen of the Andrew W. Mellon Foundation raised a key question regarding the capacity of even the wealthiest institutions in this sector to scale back on the range of their activities, to set firmer priorities, and to resist the ruthless competition for students that seems to drive so much spending on campuses. He urged leading institutions in this sector to work together to reduce wasteful aspects of competition that no one college or university could undertake on its own—in short, collusion (in spite of the chilling climate created by the antitrust case brought against several selective colleges in the early 1990s). Bowen's concern is that legal counsels to colleges and universities are stressing extremely conservative views on what the colleges can do together, and he challenged those in the audience to test those limits, in the public interest. This was a theme that echoed throughout the discussions on both days, including possibilities for public/private collaboration. Needless to say, the issue was not resolved, but by raising it in this setting, one hopes that further discussions and subsequent action may follow.

Public Institutions

On the second day of the conference, a panel of three public college and university administrators discussed the conference themes from their vantage points; these speakers included Sylvia Manning, chancellor of the University of Illinois at Chicago; Alfredo G. de los Santos, Jr., professor at Arizona State University and former administrator at Maricopa County Community Colleges; and Robert Shelton, executive administrator and provost of the University of North Carolina at Chapel Hill.

University of Illinois at Chicago: Chancellor Manning began by providing basic data about this urban campus of 25,000 students, of which 16,000 are undergraduates. She noted that UIC is largely a commuter campus, with 25 percent of its undergraduates being underrepresented minorities, 24 percent Asian, 48 percent Caucasians, and 3 percent other. With regard to financial aid, 37 percent of the undergraduates receive Pell Grants, 50 percent come from families with less than

$50,000 income, and 30 percent pay no tuition at all because of grant support. The mean SAT score of undergraduate students is about 1120, which is 200 to 300 points below the most selective institutions. For a variety of reasons, the campus experiences high rates of attrition prior to graduation, although no figure was cited.

UIC was formed in 1982 through the consolidation of two University of Illinois campuses—the Health Sciences campus, which dates to the nineteenth century, and the Chicago campus, which dates to 1965. Its medical school is the largest in the United States, and the operating budget of UIC is $1.3 billion. Sponsored research has increased rapidly to a current $250 million, and UIC is now ranked 48th among research universities by NSF in terms of annual funding. Undergraduate in-state tuition and fees totaled $7,260 for the 2004-05 academic year.

With regard to the topic of the conference, Chancellor Manning expressed a sense of what a different world she lives in from that of Amherst or Bryn Mawr. She summed up her views by noting that "I don't need a thumb on the scale to help low-income students enroll, I need a bag of gold to finance those we have." She expressed considerable concern about the declining support the campus receives from the state, the resulting upward pressure on tuition for a university that has many low-income students, and the struggle to retain high-quality faculty in the face of these budget pressures. She noted that Northwestern University (to name one of many) attempts to pick off her highest quality research faculty, and that they manage to do this when her faculty realize that all that they need to is turn the other way out of the driveway in the morning; i.e., family life is not disrupted, children do not have to change schools, and life seems more secure in the private university sector. Her major concern about higher education in the United States is that it is evolving into a two-tiered system of haves and have-nots. UIC's slogan is Access and Exellence—she fears that both objectives are threatened, given current trends in public university finance.

Maricopa County Community Colleges: Although Alfredo de los Santos, Jr. is currently a faculty member at Arizona State University, his focus was on the community college, drawing on his prior experience with MCCC. His first point was to argue that when one examines inclusiveness in American higher education, one must first and foremost focus on community colleges, where 6.6 million students were enrolled for credit in 2003, making up 46 percent of all undergraduates and 45 percent of all first-time freshmen. Furthermore, when one considers the southwestern states, where his career has unfolded, the key issue is not family income or race, but rather ethnicity, Latinos in particular. In Arizona, 75 percent of the growth in public school enrollment in the last decade has been Latino students, while in Texas, the majority of students in public schools in the largest cities—Houston, Dallas, El Paso, San Antonio, and Austin—are Latinos.

In New Mexico, Latinos will soon represent the majority of high school graduates, while California is home to the largest number of Latinos in the United States. Based on projections prepared by the Western Interstate Commission for Higher Education (WICHE), by 2017–2018, Latinos will account for more than 22 percent of all high school graduates in the United States. Thus, de los Santos concludes, when considering his region, ethnicity comes first and income comes second.

The second point he stressed had to do with academic performance and community colleges. Here the focus was on the transfer function, which has been the subject of a 50-year debate about whether community colleges contribute to opportunity or "cool" students out by lowering their aspirations and blunting their hopes. While acknowledging that the data are not always crystal clear in answering this question, he noted that the 2000-01 *Baccalaureate and Beyond Survey* compiled by the National Center for Education Statistics found that of all 1999–2000 recipients of B.A. degrees, 19.5 percent began their postsecondary education at a community college. Among Latinos, that figure was nearly one in four. Coming closer to home, he provided data from Arizona State University showing that nearly two-thirds of recent ASU graduates had attended one or more of the Maricopa County Community Colleges prior to graduating, while among Latino graduates, the figure was nearly three out of four. He made a strong case that any meaningful examination of educational opportunities beyond high school in the United States must consider the significant role played by community colleges.

University of North Carolina at Chapel Hill: Within the last two years, at least two selective public universities (with more to follow?) have announced and implemented plans to guarantee full financial aid without loans for any student admitted from a family with an income below 200 percent of the poverty level.[6] Those institutions are the University of North Carolina at Chapel Hill, with the Carolina Covenant, and the University of Virginia, with AccessUVa. Sarah Turner's essay in this volume discusses experience during the first year of AccessUVa at the University of Virginia; Provost Robert Shelton of UNC Chapel Hill provided information in his panel presentation on experience with the Carolina Covenant.

The Covenant was designed by Associate Provost Shirley Ort in 2002 in response to a question from Provost Shelton about how they could make the university accessible to academically qualified students from the lowest income

---

6. In its first year, North Carolina did use the 150 percent of poverty criterion to select the 223 students, but for subsequent years they have raised the criterion to 200 percent of poverty in order to attract more eligible students. Virginia found that at 150 percent of the poverty level too few students met that standard to make the program meaningful, and thus it begins at 200 percent.

groups. After the program was designed, however, the university could not afford to implement it without taking three additional steps: first, improved infrastructure for administering the program was essential, and was funded by the provost; second, the university needed a commitment for increased need-based aid from the state, which was provided; and third, they needed a commitment from the Board of Trustees to "hold harmless" any campus-based tuition increase that they approved, and that policy was established. With these pieces in place, the Covenant was announced in 2003 and implemented for the entering class in 2004.

The Covenant pledges that the university will meet 100 percent of an admitted, eligible student's financial need with a combination of grants, scholarships, and a reasonable amount of federal work-study income. Recipients who participate in work-study will not need to take out loans to meet financial need. Both in-state and out-of-state students are eligible for this program, and 223 enrolled during its first year. As noted earlier, eligibility is limited to students from families with incomes at or below 200 percent of the federal poverty guidelines, which for a family of four in 2005–2006 means an income of $37,700 or lower. Consideration for this award is automatic upon completion of an admitted student's financial aid application.

Of the 223 first year enrollees, average parental income was $13,400 and average high school GPA was 4.21. Average SAT scores for this group was 1209, compared to 1287 for all freshmen. Sixty percent were students of color, 55 percent were first-generation college students, and 21 percent were first-generation high school graduates. Most are in-state students (87 percent), and 69 percent are female. It seems apparent that this program is hitting the target group that Bowen et al. discuss in their book. The provost estimated in June 2005 that 350 new students would enroll in the fall entering class.

It was noted earlier that President Henry Bienen argues that all students regardless of family income should undertake some loan obligation as part of a financial package, a view shared by many policy analysts as well. Shelton explained, however, that the university sought a clear, simple message that low-income students can afford to attend Chapel Hill, and being able to say that no debt is required helps get that message out. In the early years of such a program a no-loan policy may be necessary, if inefficient, and perhaps down the road can be modified modestly to introduce some loan financing. The university also made a key marketing decision by calling the recipients Covenant Scholars, thus making the award an honor rather than a sign of low income only.

It is interesting that, even though the academic profile of the Covenant Scholars is strong, the university has invested in several programs to provide extra academic support, including a summer orientation program and paid faculty mentoring. Thus far the students are faring well, with a strong increase in GPA from the fall to the spring semester. Of the initial 223 students, 14 had grades that threatened their eligibility, and they are being offered special summer courses to help raise their GPAs, at a cost of $150,000 to the university. The program will also include eligible transfer students as the full four classes are sequentially enrolled.

The incremental cost of the program has not been that large, as such students would have received full financial aid awards in the past, with the only difference being the replacements of loans with work-study funds. For the program in 2005-06, the university estimates the program will cost $3 million over the base, of which 52 percent is estimated to come from federal sources, 10 percent from state sources, and 38 percent from institutional funds. Other costs include increased administrative burdens, consulting expenses, freshman orientation ($45,000), faculty mentoring ($96,000), and summer courses ($150,000). The university has also launched a fund-raising campaign to raise private support for Covenant scholarships.

It should be noted that for both the North Carolina and Virginia plans, the high academic selectivity of the universities means that even with these full financial packages, the number of students who are eligible remains relatively modest. One need only compare the numbers of supported students cited above with what would be involved at the University of Illinois at Chicago or at Maricopa County Community Colleges to realize that only a select few public universities will have the combination of sufficient institutional wealth and high academic selectivity that makes such programs financially feasible. Nonetheless, the North Carolina and Virginia programs are noble efforts and well worth studying to determine their true impacts, strengths, and weaknesses.

Discussion: The public college and university panel provoked a number of questions that had not arisen earlier in the conference. Because public universities maintain out-of-state tuition differentials that are often quite large, a number of people were surprised that both the North Carolina and Virginia plans included out-of-state students in the eligible population. One suspects that most state political leaders would have minimal interest in seeing their state institutions provide full financial aid packages for students from other states, particularly if such aid is viewed (rightly or wrongly) as coming at the expense of in-state students. Thus far, both institutions seem not to be saying much publicly about the number of out-of-state students supported, and only time will tell whether that issue becomes a bone of contention. A further issue involved how such programs can be made to serve low-income students who do not follow a straight path to the flagship university, but instead enroll in multiple institutions along the way, a pattern referred to as "swirling" by Alfredo de los Santos, Jr. Others wondered why and to what extent special enrichment programs were needed for students who qualify for admission under established academic criteria. A question was also raised as to the potential stigmatizing effect of advertising that certain students were Covenant Scholars, which by definition identifies them as being from very low-income families. It is clear that these new programs will face numerous issues going forward but, on balance, both the North Carolina and Virginia programs appear to be off to a promising start.

Concluding Comments

Reflecting back on the six institutions, the diversity of missions, aspirations, resources, competitors, students, and opportunities described above drive home the lesson that no single approach to increased socioeconomic diversity will work for all campuses. In a few privileged cases, the resources and potential student populations are there, and the key issue will be the values held by decision makers and the tradeoffs they perceive. In other cases (unfortunately, the vast majority), resources will remain a critical constraint, and funds devoted to additional student aid will come at the cost of core functions. The closing conversation raised these issues by focusing on a question of values: Is increased socioeconomic diversity compatible with prestige or quality maximizing behavior at the institutional level? For many institutions, students from low-income families will not raise the academic profile of the student body and, indeed, may lower it modestly—is that a cost institutions are willing to bear, particularly when coupled with the additional financial outlays required to support such students? No easy answer to this central value question seems apparent. In the absence of publicly available data on income distributions by campus, it will be impossible to determine the extent to which institutions have responded to this challenge.

The seeds of this conference were sown by the availability of such detailed data for 19 highly selective colleges and universities, a unique data set assembled by the Andrew W. Mellon Foundation. With that database, Bowen et al. were able to undertake the analyses that revealed the striking absence of low-income, first-generation college students in these 19 schools, despite their presence in the applicant pools. Because the 19 schools are not a representative sample of the nation's colleges and universities, an obvious issue that arose in a corridor conversation was whether it would be feasible to collect a comparable data set for a more diverse sample of schools. One hopes that conversation will move forward, and that the project will prove feasible, for then it may be possible to monitor enrollment trends by income at the campus level in ways that currently cannot be measured.

Other issues reprised in the concluding discussion included the focus on K–12 improvement, which everyone agreed is a critical constraint on academic preparation that bears disproportionately upon the poor. Variants on the issue that Anthony Marx raised were also mentioned, in that several participants wondered to what extent these issues represent a zero-sum game, and to what extent there are potential gains for the public good. And finally, the issue raised by William Bowen regarding opportunities and challenges for cooperation and collaboration as opposed to competition continued to be brought up. The limitations on what a single college or university can do if others do not follow gives rise to potential efficiency and equity gains if cooperative behavior can be established. Perhaps that overarching issue will be the focus for the next Macalester conference.

Section III:
Getting In and
Getting Through

Maximizing Opportunity: Steering Underrepresented Students Through the Selective College Persistence Tracks

Michael T. Nettles and Catherine M. Millett

Introduction

While the legal and political challenges to higher education admissions practices affect all of America's colleges and universities, the nation's 173 most selective are at the core of the dispute.[1] Judicial proceedings and political campaigns in California, Michigan, Texas, and Washington exposed the considerable investment that selective colleges and universities are making in order to expand access. Though the scales of justice and public opinion remain tilted heavily in the favor of high socioeconomic and majority students, selective colleges and universities have tried to admit and graduate more diverse classes of students.

The evidence of representation by race/ethnicity is clear. African American and Hispanic students now represent roughly 6 percent each in the entering freshman classes of the most selective colleges and universities (see Table 1). Although this is less than half their representation in the general population of the age group (14 percent each), it is substantial.

Table 1. First-time, full-time freshmen attending four-year or more colleges and universities, by selectivity: fall 2003 (Institutional N=1,411)

	Total	African American	Asian American	Hispanic	White
U.S. Pop. Age 18–24 (2000)	26,541,000	3,810,000	1,038,000	3,956,000	17,496,000
		14.4%	3.9%	14.9%	65.9%
Enrollment in Institutions with 4-year or more programs (Institutional N=2595)	1,379,267	155,119	80,855	99,957	934,731
		11.2%	5.9%	7.2%	67.8%
Most Comp. (69)	88,019	5,761	12,939	6,496	52,506
		6.5%	14.7%	7.4%	59.7%
Highly Comp. (102)	144,123	7,235	14,652	9,322	101,460
		5.0%	10.2%	6.5%	70.4%

Note: Institutional selectivity is based on *Barron's Profiles of American Colleges 2005.* Not available for all institutions; U.S. population data are from the *Statistical Abstract of the United States: 2001*, Table 17; enrollment data are from the IPEDS 2003 Enrollment file.

---

1. Please refer to *Barron's Profiles of American Colleges 2005* (Hauppauge, N.Y.: Barron's Educational Series, 2004) for the most competitive and highly competitive colleges and universities.

For the 1995 entering cohort in the 19 institutions in the Bowen, Kurzweil, and Tobin study,[2] applicants from the bottom family national quartile of income comprised 11.7 percent of applicants, 9.1 percent of admitted students, 11.8 percent of enrolled students, and 10.6 percent of the graduates. The students who are first-generation college students comprised 6.5 percent of applicants, 5.4 percent of admitted students, 6.2 percent of enrolled students, and 6.1 percent of graduates.

The continuing underrepresentation in entering classes at selective colleges reflects the underrepresentation of African American and Hispanic students among the best academically prepared students. But, it also reflects the caution upon which colleges and universities proceed in response to two constant arguments advanced by opponents of broader access through admissions:

- First, that systems of merit that favor underrepresented minority and low-socioeconomic status candidates over their majority and wealthy contemporaries are unconstitutional; and

- Second, that relatively high socioeconomic status and majority students are more successful completing curriculum requirements and benefit more from the educational experience in selective colleges and universities than their African American, Hispanic, and low-socioeconomic status contemporaries.

Both arguments attack the short-term strategies of colleges and universities to expand access through admissions. Both are captured in the following comment by ardent opponents of action about the actions of proponents of affirmative action by colleges and universities to broaden access through the admissions process:

> However benevolent the motives of such progressive thinkers, their muddled thinking has had unfortunate consequences, as we saw with the University of Illinois example. The risk in taking in a "high risk" student like Fred Abernathy is that of academic failure. When it does not work out, the loser is not the institution but the individual student, who suffers a crushing, humiliating personal defeat that may have lasting results. That should be of special concern when the student (who might be fine at a less competitive school) has already been scarred by encounters with racial prejudice.[3]

---

2. William G. Bowen, Martin A. Kurzweil, and Eugene M. Tobin, *Equity and Excellence in American Higher Education* (Charlottesville, Va.: University of Virginia Press, 2005), 95–136.

3. Stephan Thernstrom and Abigail Thernstrom, *America in Black and White: One Nation, Indivisible* (New York: Simon & Schuster, 1977), 395.

To address this position, concrete evidence is needed about the persistence and completion of underrepresented students in selective colleges and universities compared to their more privileged contemporaries.

What are the race and social class differences in persistence, stop-out, and transfer rates of undergraduate students attending selective colleges and universities and the factors that contribute to these outcomes? For this study the following operational definitions are employed: (a) persister—a student who is enrolled or graduates from the institution where she enrolled as a first-time, full-time freshman, (b) stop-out—a student who is not continuously enrolled at the institution where she enrolled as a first-time, full-time freshman, (c) transfer—a student who self-reported that she had left her original college and enrolled at a different one.

Two important questions to consider are the following:

- What are the race and social class differences in the persistence of students in selective college and universities?

- What are the experiences of students that account for their persistence?

One of the long-standing and most frequent topics of research on higher education is college student attrition. For more than a half century, social and behavioral scientists have examined the issue of student attrition, transfer, and persistence in college but have rarely focused on race and social class in selective colleges and universities. Still, much can be learned from the history of research on student persistence that can be applied to the study of race and social class in selective colleges. Although this essay is too brief to attempt to thoroughly cover the rich history of research on college student persistence, a small sampling provides both perspective and context for the procedures and the content of the present study.

Among the earliest research focusing on the target population of selective colleges and universities was Alexander Astin's longitudinal study of National Merit Scholars in 1964. Astin estimated that 10 percent of the students had dropped out, stopped out, or transferred by 1961, and the rest had graduated. Astin's reason for excluding race as a focus may have been the paucity of ethnic diversity among PSAT/NMSQT® takers in the subsample of the National Merit Scholars pool and the absence of race as a central issue in student persistence in the middle of the twentieth century when he conducted the research. For whatever reason race was excluded, this began a trend of exclusion in persistence research that continued through much of the next five decades. The omission of race notwithstanding, Astin made some interesting discoveries regarding performance and personality characteristics that distinguished persisters from nonpersisters. He concluded that "students who dropped out of college before receiving a baccalaureate degree come from lower socioeconomic status backgrounds, had lower ranks in high school, plan initially to get lower college degrees, and apply for relatively fewer scholarships than do students who do not drop out."[4] Personality measures suggested that dropouts tended to be more aloof, self-centered, impulsive, and assertive than nondropouts. The only institutional effect that Astin found was that women who attended institutions where there were a relatively large share of men tended to drop out at a higher rate.

After reviewing research from two prior decades, William Spady developed a theoretical model in which he hypothesized relationships among a variety of student and institutional characteristics with student achievement and attrition.[5] The following year, Spady tested his model with data that he gathered from the students themselves and from the university about the students who entered the University of Chicago in 1966.[6] Spady's pioneering work illuminates the importance of the distinction between the role played by social psychological measures such as friendship support and positive attitudes about academics and by academic preparation. The former (social psychological measures) is a more important predictor of students' intellectual development and attrition, while the latter (academic preparation) is more predictive of student academic performance in college. Spady concluded that indeed the more academically competitive a student's high school is, the stronger her/his high school performance, and the higher her/his mathematical and verbal aptitude, the greater the student's chances of meeting the academic demands of the college. But, Spady also concluded that these same characteristics have less bearing upon persistence than a student's interpersonal contacts, dating relationships, and social integration into the college.[7]

Fast-forward 40 years in the research on student persistence. Bowen and his colleagues, Kurzweil and Tobin, were surprised to find that students from families of modest incomes and parental educational attainment were not markedly different from their affluent and middle-class contemporaries in the likelihood of them being admitted, enrolling, and completing degrees as long as they were adequately prepared in school prior to entering college. Based upon these estimates, Bowen, Kurzweil, and Tobin concluded that while such students are in short supply, they are not short on success in the nation's most selective colleges and universities. While Bowen, Kurzweil, and Tobin inform us about the effects of a social class, they do not address race.[8]

---

4. A. W. Astin, "Personal and Environmental Factors Associated with College Dropouts Among High-Aptitude Students," *Journal of Educational Psychology* 55 (1964): 219–227.

5. William G. Spady, "Dropouts from Higher Education: An Interdisciplinary Review and Synthesis," *Interchange* 1, No. 1 (1970): 64–85.

6. William G. Spady, "Dropouts from Higher Education: Toward an Empirical Model," *Interchange* 2, No. 3 (1971): 38–62.

7. Ibid., 59.

8. Bowen, Kurzweil, and Tobin, *Equity and Excellence in American Higher Education.*

Sample Selection, Survey Methodology and Interviews

This essay is based on a survey of undergraduate student persisters, stop-outs, and transfers in 15 selective colleges and universities in the United States (see Table 2). The 15 universities comprise a vital component of a larger purposive sample of colleges and universities that followed the design of the Andrew W. Mellon Foundation study, *College and Beyond.*[9]

The student sample was designed to be representative of student persisters and leavers. The leavers were later divided into stop-outs and transfers. The students who were included in the student sample were (1) first-time, full-time freshmen who enrolled in 1996, 1997, or 1998; (2) were at least 18 years old but not older than 25;[10] (3) were U.S. citizens or permanent residents;[11] and (4) were African American, Asian American, Hispanic/Latino, or white.

The *Survey of College Choices, Experiences, and Retention* (*SOCCER*), developed by Nettles and Millett in 1999, was used for this study. A persister and a stop-out version of *SOCCER* were developed. There is a common body of questions for both surveys and then each version has additional questions unique to their respective experiences. The common elements consist of three sections: (1) application and enrollment process at the first college or university, (2) student experiences at their original college, and (3) student background. The stop-out version has additional questions regarding students' experiences after departing and the persister version has additional questions about the college experience. The overall response rate is 45 percent.

Table 2: Participating colleges and universities in the high-achieving college student persistence study

Bryn Mawr	University of California at Los Angeles
Cornell University	University of Michigan
Lehigh University	University of North Carolina
Macalester College	University of Pennsylvania
Northwestern University	Wellesley College
Oberlin College	Wesleyan University
Rice University	Williams College
Tulane University	

Source: Nettles and Millett, *Survey of College Choices, Experiences, and Retention* (1999).

9. William G. Bowen and Derek Bok, *The Shape of the River: Long-Term Consequences of Considering Race in College and University Admissions* (Princeton, N.J.: Princeton University Press, 1998).

10. When the institution provided the age of students.

11. When the institution was able to provide the information.

The Variables

Variables were selected for inclusion in the quantitative analyses on the basis of their fit into the following eight categories: (1) personal background (gender, race, family income, and parents' highest level of education), (2) college admissions (SAT score), (3) college academic experiences (grades in college, academic compatibility, academic time management, faculty support, faculty interaction, and instructional quality), (4) perceived discrimination (experienced discrimination and racial climate), (5) social experiences (social compatibility and supportive environment), (6) worrying about financing a college degree (financial concerns), (7) educational commitment (college belonging, institutional satisfaction, and commitment to their college or university), and (8) student's self-concept. The dependent variable for this study is enrollment status. Originally the participating colleges and universities provided enrollment information that allowed us to determine if a student should receive a persister or nonpersister survey.

Student Interviews

In addition to the surveys that the students completed, we wanted to hear from them in their own words about their experiences at their college or university. We invited students who were persisters, stop-outs, and transfers to talk with us at selected cities and campuses across the country. We conducted 163 semistructured interviews with students. The goals of the interviews were to understand the meaning of events and actions as expressed by the students about their college experiences, backgrounds, plans, and aspirations. The idea is to describe the students' points of view and to learn how they thought about their experiences, as well as how they interpret and explain their behavior and experiences in college.

Findings

Statistical Analyses

The findings are presented to address these two questions: Are there class and race and differences in persistence rates? What factors account for the differences?

Persisters, Transfers, and Stop-Outs

The overall rates of better than 90 percent of persisters are consistent with research findings dating back through the past half-century on selective colleges and universities. The persistence rates of students in four ranges of family income are consistent with the findings of Bowen, Kurzweil, and Tobin who found no significant difference.[12] In the lowest of the four income ranges, below $50,000, 88 percent were persisters, compared to between 92 percent and 93 percent in the other three income ranges. Around 8 percent of the students in the lowest income range transferred to other universities and 3 percent stopped out without transferring, compared to around 5 percent and 3 percent, respectively, of the other three income categories.

The race/ethnic differences are statistically significant (p=.037) but not large, with African Americans at 89 percent, Asian Americans at 94 percent, Hispanics at 90 percent, and whites at 92 percent. Around 6 percent of the African Americans and 8 percent of the Hispanics transferred, and 5 percent and 3 percent, respectively, stopped out without transferring. Among Asian American students, 4 percent transferred and 2 percent stopped out; and among white students, 6 percent transferred and 2 percent stopped out.

Predictors of Persisters Versus Stop-Outs

Among the variables examined in this study, seven were identified that distinguish persisters from stop-outs. Persisters are found to achieve higher undergraduate GPAs, are less satisfied with their institutions, display less concern about their finances, have a stronger commitment to their institutions, have a greater amount of interaction with faculty, and are academically more compatible with their institutions, but they have a lower quality of academic time management. Race was found to not be a significant factor in persistence when these seven and other factors were taken into account.

Predictors of Transfers Versus Stop-Outs

Four characteristics were found to distinguish transfers from stop-outs. Transfers had a higher degree of academic compatibility with their institutions, had stronger academic time management, had a lower quality of interaction with faculty, and had a lower commitment to their institution. As with comparing persisters to stop-outs, race was not a factor in distinguishing transfers from stop-outs.

Part of a Selected Interview

One persister's experience depicts some of the challenges faced by under-represented students. Brendan, an African American male persister, is a first-generation student from a low-socioeconomic status family. He achieved a relatively low SAT score.

---

12. Bowen, Kurzweil, and Tobin, *Equity and Excellence in American Higher Education.*

"I took the SAT once. My plan was not to go to college. I did not think about college first. Because of my SAT score (1050) and because of all these issues, especially since that year affirmative action was kicked out here, so I didn't think I had too much of a chance to get into college.

"I wasn't going to apply to college but my science teacher encouraged me to apply to college. I couldn't do it on my own because I couldn't afford it."

When asked about the transition to college, Brendan told us:

"It was difficult. It was very, very difficult. I felt so many feelings of inadequacy before I even came here because the school I came from already watered down grades. I was like...I don't think I'm prepared. In fact, I wasn't...One of my first papers I got a D on. That was really discouraging. I had to push through. I had to adjust because I didn't know anybody. It was hard because I had people prodding me about not going. Like, 'You'll flunk out.'

"I worked really, really hard. I studied a lot...I thought I was doing pretty well in that class and then come back to find out I got a D+. After I got a D+ I think that was when my perception changed. I was focused on making sure I'd never get another D or anything like that. That's when I really began to question (my ability) and really come to terms with the reasons for being here. I had to definitely define some reasons for being here. After all, if I'm going to think to myself, 'Why am I here? What do I really want to get out of the school? Am I here just because everyone said I could go to college?' It took me about a year to figure it out. When I figured it out it was revelation."

Brendan's college experience turned around. Later in our interview Brendan shared a brighter moment in his academic life with us.

"There's such a high standard in the class and I got an A-. That was my first quarter. That set the tone for me. That let me know that I can make it here, that I'm actually capable. My high school counselors would say, 'If you made it into CalSouth, then obviously you must be CalSouth material.' I didn't feel like CalSouth material. When I got my A- in my political science class, I said, 'Hey, that's great for me.' I wrote my papers. I got a lot of help. I got tutoring to help out. I went to speak with my professors who were really cool."

Conclusion

Like other measures of college performance, race and social class equality in student persistence depends upon quality of preparation for college. But collegiate experience is important to an even greater extent than preparation and student experience. The race difference in student persistence that is observed by simply comparing the rates is minute and there are no observable race differences in transferring/stopping out.

The fact that college grades are the biggest predictor of persisting versus stopping out is not surprising but, when controlling for grades, student background characteristics play a very minor role in predicting college student persistence. The additional elements of success in persisting for underrepresented students are having positive and high quality interactions with faculty, seeking compatibility with the academic aspects of the institution, and developing a strong commitment and allegiance to the institution. Brendan displayed all three of these behaviors in his quest to succeed.

Claiming Common Ground: State Policymaking
for Improving College Readiness and Success

Patrick M. Callan, Joni E. Finney, Michael W. Kirst, Michael D. Usdan, and Andrea Venezia

Introduction

Major demographic shifts in the population of the United States, combined with persistent gaps in educational achievement by ethnic groups, could decrease the portion of the workforce with college-level skills over the next 15 years, with a consequent decline in per capita personal income in the United States.[1] Meanwhile, the competitive edge of the U.S. workforce is slipping; several other developed countries now surpass the United States in the percentage of their young working-age population enrolling in college and attaining a bachelor's degree.[2] At a time when the knowledge-based global economy requires more Americans with education and training beyond high school, the nation confronts the prospect of a sustained drop in the average educational levels of the U.S. workforce.[3] This challenge places the United States at a crossroads: We can improve college readiness and completion rates and thereby prepare the workforce for the economic and civic challenges of the next generation, or we can allow gaps in educational achievement to undermine our competitive edge and our communities' economic prosperity.

Leaders from throughout the country—in public and private schools, charter schools, foundations, educational and policy organizations, businesses, states, and the federal government—have taken up this challenge. For example, reforming high schools has become a major focus in an overall drive to raise student achievement. Many of these efforts to improve our secondary schools have targeted student readiness for both college and work as a single key objective; the skills and knowledge required for middle-income jobs closely mirror those required for college success. As research has documented, reforms that focus either on K–12 schools or on colleges and universities are likely to perpetuate some of the key barriers to improving educational achievement for students.[4] Yet the focus of most state education reforms

1. National Center for Public Policy and Higher Education, "Income of U.S. Workforce Projected to Decline if Education Doesn't Improve," *Policy Alert* (Nov. 2005).

2. Organisation for Economic Co-operation and Development (OECD), *Education at a Glance* (Paris, France: 2004).

3. Patrick Kelly, *As America Becomes More Diverse: The Impact of State Higher Education Inequality* (Boulder, Colo.: National Center for Higher Education Management Systems, 2005).

4. Andrea Venezia, Michael Kirst, and Anthony Antonio, *Betraying the College Dream: How Disconnected K–12 and Postsecondary Education Systems Undermine Student Aspirations* (Stanford, Cal.: Bridge Project, Stanford Institute for Higher Education Research, 2003).

has been limited to K–12 school systems. Some of the most robust challenges in raising student achievement can be found at the juncture—or more accurately the disjuncture—between our K–12 systems and our colleges and universities.

In the United States, secondary education and postsecondary education have developed divergent histories, governance structures, policies, and institutional boundaries. As a result, there are few widespread practices or traditions for these two systems of education to communicate with each other, much less to collaborate to improve student achievement across institutions. Advocacy organizations are working on behalf of K–12 schools on the one hand or on behalf of colleges and universities on the other, but there are no lobbying groups in state capitals seeking to improve college readiness by bridging the divide between K–12 and higher education. There are few accountability systems that track college readiness from secondary to postsecondary education. And no one is held responsible for the students who fall between the cracks of the two systems.

Gaining admission to college is not the most daunting challenge facing high school graduates—although many students think that it is and most college-preparation efforts focus on admissions. The more difficult challenge for students is becoming prepared academically for college course work. Once students enter college, about half of them learn that they are not prepared for college-level courses. Forty percent of students at four-year institutions and 63 percent at two-year colleges take remedial education.[5] According to *Measuring Up 2004*, the state-by-state report card on higher education, the timely completion of certificates and degrees remains one of the weakest aspects of performance in higher education.[6]

This essay identifies four state policy dimensions for improving college-readiness opportunities for all high school students:

- **Alignment of course work and assessments:** States should require K–12 and postsecondary education to align their courses and assessments. Currently, the K–12 standards movement and efforts to improve access and success in higher education are not connected.

- **State finance:** States should develop financial incentives and support to stimulate K–12 and postsecondary education to collaborate to improve college readiness and success. Most existing state finance systems perpetuate the divide between K–12 and postsecondary education.

---

5. National Center for Education Statistics, *The Condition of Education* (Washington, D.C.: U.S. Department of Education, 2001), 148.

6. National Center for Public Policy and Higher Education, *Measuring Up 2004* (Sept. 2004), www.highereducation.org.

- **Statewide data systems:** States should develop the capacity to track students across educational institutions statewide. Currently, most states do not collect adequate data to address the effectiveness of K–12 reforms in improving student readiness for college.

- **Accountability:** States should publicly report on student progress and success from high school through postsecondary education. Schools, colleges, and universities should be held accountable for improving student performance from high school to college completion.

Through these policy levers, states can create the conditions for claiming common ground between our systems of K–12 and postsecondary education.

Context and Findings

Many forces are converging to create a pressing need for state policies to improve college readiness and success. For example, the fastest growing job sectors in our economy require workers to have at least some education or training beyond high school.[7] Yet completion rates for associate and bachelor's degree programs have stalled over the past decade, and wide gaps remain in college completion by ethnic and income groups.[8] Whereas the United States was once the world leader in offering college opportunity to its residents, several countries have now overtaken the United States in this area. The educational attainment of the young workforce (ages 24 to 34) in the United States currently ranks fifth among industrialized nations.[9]

Unless the educational achievement of the young population improves, the competitiveness of the U.S. workforce is projected to decline over the next decades. Economists Anthony Carnevale and Donna Desrochers have estimated that by 2020 the United States could face a shortfall of 14 million workers who have the knowledge and skills needed to compete for middle-income jobs in a global economy.[10] In addition, recent population studies have found that unless states can improve the education of all students, the percentage of the U.S. workforce with a bachelor's degree will decrease over the next 15 years, with a corresponding drop in personal income per capita. Minority groups with the

7. Anthony Carnevale and Donna Desrochers, *Standards for What? The Economic Roots of K–16 Reform* (Princeton, N.J.: Educational Testing Service, 2003), http://www.ets.org/research/dload/standards_for_what.pdf.

8. National Center for Public Policy and Higher Education, *Measuring Up 2000*, *Measuring Up 2002*, and *Measuring Up 2004* (2000, 2002, 2004), www.highereducation.org.

9. OECD, *Education at a Glance*.

10. Carnevale and Desrochers, *Standards for What?*

lowest average levels of education will grow rapidly, while the baby boomers—the most highly educated generation in U.S. history—are expected to retire in record numbers. From 1980 to 2020, the minority portion of the workforce is projected to double from 18 percent to 37 percent, and the Hispanic/Latino portion will almost triple, from 6 percent to 17 percent. During the same period, the white working-age population is projected to decline from 82 percent to 63 percent.[11]

Educators and policymakers have known since the 1980s that this country would need a more highly educated workforce. For the past several decades, they have broadcast a consistent message urging high school students to attend college—and students have responded. Today's high school students have higher academic aspirations than ever before; almost 90 percent of high school students of all racial and ethnic groups aspire to attend college. Almost 60 percent of high school graduates enroll in college right after high school,[12] and many additional students enroll in college within a few years of high school graduation. But educators and policymakers have not fulfilled their side of the bargain; they have not developed coherent state systems of education that adequately prepare high school students for the academic expectations of college. High school students who want to enroll in college must navigate a maze of disconnected curricula and assessments that are reinforced by state policies that are themselves unconnected and often at cross purposes with one another.[13] These fractured and fragmented systems waste taxpayer money on duplicated and inefficient uses of resources, they create barriers for high school students who want to prepare for college, and they undermine efforts to improve college completion rates. The K–12 and postsecondary education systems in the United States should be working together to improve college readiness and success, yet our nation's education systems remain sharply divided.

Leaks in the Pipeline

Despite the high educational aspirations of high school students, the United States has low and inequitable high school graduation and college completion rates. About two-thirds of ninth-graders (68 percent) graduate from high school within four years. And less than one-fifth of ninth-graders (18 percent) finish

11. National Center for Public Policy and Higher Education, "Income of U.S. Workforce Projected to Decline."

12. Tom Mortenson, "Chance for College by Age 19 by State 1986 to 2002," *Postsecondary Education OPPORTUNITY* No. 149 (Nov. 2004): 10.

13. Michael Kirst and Andrea Venezia (eds.), *From High School to College: Improving Opportunities for Success in Postsecondary Education* (San Francisco: Jossey-Bass, 2004).

high school within four years, go on to college right after graduation, and then complete either an associate degree within three years of enrolling or a bachelor's degree within six years.[14] In examining student progress from high school to college, there are also large gaps between ethnic groups (see Figure 1). Almost a quarter (23 percent) of white students receive an associate degree within three years or a bachelor's degree within six years of enrolling in college. In contrast, only 9 percent of African Americans and 10 percent of Hispanic/Latinos do so.[15]

There is also a very large educational divide by income in the United States. For those high school graduates from the wealthiest quartile (25 percent) of the overall population, about two of every three enroll in a four-year college or

Figure 1. U.S. educational pipeline by race/ethnicity

Of 100 ninth-graders, how many...

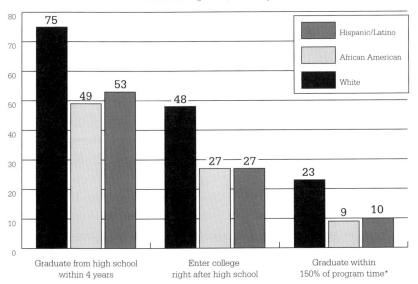

*150 percent of program time is three years for those seeking an associate degree and six years for those seeking a bachelor's degree.

Note: These "educational pipeline" data are from 2001. The analysis is not a longitudinal study that tracks a sample of students over time. It is developed based on a combination of several national data sources that measure student success rates at each transition point. Due to data limitations, it does not account for transfer students.

Sources: Analysis by National Center for Higher Education Management Systems (www.higheredinfo.org), based on data from NCES Common Core Data; *IPEDS 2002 Fall Enrollment Survey; IPEDS 2002 Graduation Rate Survey*

14. National Center for Public Policy and Higher Education, "The Educational Pipeline: Big Investment, Big Returns," *Policy Alert* (April 2004).

15. National Center for Education Statistics, Common Core Data, "IPEDS 2002 Fall Enrollment Survey" and "IPEDS 2002 Graduation Rate Survey," Early Release Data (Washington, D.C.: U.S. Department of Education, 2002).

university. In contrast, only about one in five from the lowest socioeconomic quartile enrolls in a four-year institution. At the nation's most selective colleges and universities, about three-quarters of the student body are from the top socioeconomic quartile and only three percent are from the poorest quartile.[16]

Standards for College Readiness Are Confusing

From the students' perspective, the divide between high school and college is very real, even for those who plan to attend a community college. Community colleges, which enroll about 44 percent of undergraduate students,[17] have multiple missions and most admit any student over age 18 who applies and who can benefit from instruction. Since these and other broad-access institutions do not have stringent admissions requirements, many high school students assume that they do not need rigorous academic preparation. They do not understand that, as with four-year colleges and universities, community colleges have academic standards for taking college-level courses and completing a certificate or degree program.[18] After students enroll in college, they learn that they must take placement exams to determine if they qualify for college-level work or if they must take remedial courses first. About half the college students in the United States are required to enroll in remedial education.[19] This percentage could be reduced dramatically if high schools and colleges were to connect their standards, assessments, policies, and course work.

The disjunctures between high schools and postsecondary education manifest themselves in many ways. For example, high school assessments often emphasize different knowledge and skills than do college entrance and placement requirements. College placement tests for math often include Algebra II, while the assessments required for admission rarely exceed Algebra I.[20] In addition, much of the course work in high school does not build toward college readiness. For example, a recent ACT study found that high school teachers consider grammar and usage skills to be the least important writing skills, and only 69 percent of high school teachers reported that they teach grammar and usage.[21] In contrast, the study also found that college

---

16. R. D. Kahlenberg, *America's Untapped Resource: Low Income Students in Higher Education* (New York: Twentieth Century Fund, 2004).

17. National Center for Education Statistics, "Enrollment in Postsecondary Institutions" and "Financial Statistics Fiscal Year 2002" (Washington, D.C.: U.S. Department of Education, 2002).

18. Kirst and Venezia (eds.), *From High School to College.*

19. National Center for Education Statistics, *The Condition of Education*, 148.

20. The Education Trust, "Ticket to Nowhere. The Gap Between Leaving High School and Entering College and High Performance Jobs," *Thinking K–16* 3, No. 2 (Fall 1999).

21. http://www.act.org/news/releases/2003/pdf/english.pdf.

instructors consider these skills to be the most important writing skills for incoming students. Given the need to improve student achievement in high school and college, it would make sense for college and university systems to communicate extensively with high schools about what students need to know and to be able to do in order to succeed in college. But the vast majority of high school teachers receive no information from colleges about their admissions and placement standards and policies.[22]

Few Reforms Address College Readiness

Traditionally, states have viewed high schools as performing two primary tasks: preparing some students for postsecondary education and preparing most students for work. Although that division may have been appropriate decades ago, it is no longer relevant today, primarily because of the increasing technological and educational demands of the contemporary workplace. The knowledge and skills that students need to succeed in postsecondary education are equivalent to the ones they need in the workforce. As a result, some high schools are aiming for a new primary goal: to create an educational environment that provides all students with the knowledge and skills they need to succeed in education and training beyond high school.

Improving student readiness for college does not mean that every student will want or need to complete four years of a traditional liberal arts education. Some will become employed or join the military directly after high school, and many will qualify, based on their skills, for training on the job. Many high school graduates will enroll in and complete certificates or other training programs. And many will finish several years of postsecondary education, completing an associate or a bachelor's degree. No matter which career paths students choose, the completion of a high school diploma should prepare them for existing opportunities for education and training beyond high school. The diploma should also provide their prospective employers and college admissions officers with the assurance that students have attained college-ready knowledge and skills. This can only occur if public policies for K–12 and postsecondary education converge upon a common set of goals.

Since the 1980s, states have concentrated substantial resources on the reform of K–12 schools. Many of these reforms have focused on the development of statewide standards and the assessment of student achievement based on those standards. Yet most standards-setting activities—such as high school exit exams—end at the tenth-grade level, which does not represent adequate preparation for college. For example, states that have a high school graduation assessment based

---

22. Venezia, Kirst, and Antonio, *Betraying the College Dream.*

on minimum standards may be undermining their college-readiness efforts by sending mixed signals to students about what it takes to graduate from high school and succeed in college.

Recently, several national reforms focusing on college readiness, including the American Diploma Project and initiatives springing from the policy discussions at the 2005 National Education Summit sponsored by the National Governors Association and Achieve, have been under way. A consensus is emerging around a central goal: to prepare all high school graduates to engage successfully in college-level academic work.

Recommendations

The federal government, local school districts, and colleges and universities have important roles to serve in developing educational policy and practice. College-readiness reform, however, is primarily a state-level policy responsibility. As the entities that perform the major funding and policy-setting functions for public K–12 and higher education, states are in a unique position to create and adopt policies that require the systems of education to collaborate to improve college readiness and success. Currently, most collaborations between schools and colleges can be described as voluntary, localized efforts that are dependent upon ad hoc leadership commitments. States that are seeking to improve college readiness and success must move their educational systems beyond localized collaborations by taking action in four key areas of statewide policy: alignment of course work and assessments, state finance, statewide data systems, and accountability. If states are not using their policy levers in at least these four areas to align K–12 and postsecondary education, they cannot expect significant improvements in college readiness and success.

Alignment of Course Work and Assessments
States Should Require K–12 and Postsecondary Education to Align Their Course Work and Assessments.

Requiring K–12 and postsecondary education to work together to align their course work and assessments is a key step to improving college readiness. Currently, the K–12 standards movement and efforts to improve access and success in higher education are operating on different tracks. For example, a widespread K–12 reform strategy has been to increase enrollments in college-preparatory courses. Yet despite some successes in this area, remediation rates in college remain high and college completion rates remain low. As a nation, we are learning that the number of courses that high school students take, and the units and names assigned to them, are often inadequate indicators for whether high school graduates are prepared to succeed in college-level work. The quality and level of the course work and instruction, and their level of alignment with postsecondary expectations, are the key elements of reform. Making improvements in these areas require colleges and universities to participate in the new wave of high school reforms, so that new standards and curricula in high school are linked to what students need to know and be able to do in college.

High school assessments provide another example of the multiple ways students receive mixed messages about the skills they need to develop for college. High school graduation tests in most states are benchmarked at the eighth-, ninth-, and tenth-grade levels. There are few standards developed for the eleventh or twelfth grades or connected to the academic expectations of college. In June 2005, the *Boston Globe* reported that in Massachusetts "37 percent of incoming freshmen from public high schools had to take a remedial course in reading, writing, or math last year, down only two percentage points from 2002, the year before the MCAS English and math tests [the statewide tenth-grade assessments] became a graduation requirement."[23]

High school students should receive diagnostic information through assessments at key intervals in high school—well before entering college—concerning their preparation for college-level academic work, so that they can change their course-taking patterns and improve their college readiness. In order for this to take place, states must require K–12 and postsecondary education to align their assessments—for example, by aligning high school assessments with college placement tests. By taking courses and assessments that build toward college-level academic work, high school students can become better informed about and better prepared for the requirements of college.

The Early Assessment Program at California State University

As an example of promising collaborative work between K–12 and postsecondary systems, California State University (CSU) has partnered with the State Board of Education and the California Department of Education to develop the Early Assessment Program. The program was established by CSU to provide high school juniors with opportunities to measure their readiness for college-level math and English, and to help them improve their knowledge and skills during their senior year. The program's goal is to ensure that high school graduates who attend CSU are prepared to enroll and succeed in college-level courses.

---

23. Maria Sacchetti, "Colleges Question MCAS Success: Many in State Schools Still Need Remedial Help," *Boston Globe* (June 26, 2005).

The impetus for the program was the high remediation rate within CSU. To be admitted to CSU, all high school students must complete a college-preparatory curriculum and earn a grade point average of B or higher. Yet even with these requirements, about half of first-time freshmen at CSU must take remedial education in English, math, or both.[24] Based on this and other information, it became clear to CSU that the college-preparatory curriculum and grade point average requirements were not effective in developing college readiness.

Early Assessment Program Key Principles

There is a shared view of college-readiness standards across higher education.

There is a substantial core of K–12 standards and assessments that can be aligned with collegiate-readiness standards.

Postsecondary education should lead in connecting its readiness standards to K–12 standards.

K–12 standards and postsecondary education-readiness standards need to be aligned.

There needs to be direct assessment of college-readiness standards.

Additional tests and testing time should be minimized.

The timing of tests should be early enough to help students improve their preparation for college.

The work should be cost-effective.

Source: David Spence, "Early Assessment Academic Preparation Initiative," presentation at State Policy Dimensions for K–16 Reform, Wingspread Conference Center, September 12, 2005.

The Early Assessment Program includes three components: an eleventh-grade testing program, preparation opportunities for high school students, and professional development for high school teachers. The eleventh-grade assessment is part of the state's testing and accountability system, is criterion referenced, and includes items associated with twelfth-grade standards.[25] School teachers worked with university faculty to augment the California Standards Tests (end-of-course exams that all students must take) with math and English items that measure college-readiness knowledge and skills. In math, the items assess student knowledge of advanced algebra and geometry. Similarly, the English proficiency standards are aligned with the state standards in English language arts, yet require additional demonstration of advanced reading and writing skills. For example, there is a 45-minute essay requirement.

---

24. http://www.calstate.edu/eap/.

25. David Spence, "Early Assessment Academic Preparation Initiative," presentation at State Policy Dimensions for K–16 Reform, Wingspread Conference Center, September 12, 2005.

In the spring of their junior year, high school students volunteer to take the augmented sections of the California Standards Tests. The scoring of college readiness involves a combination of performance on selected items from the core tests and on the augmented items. High schools and students receive scores by early August, prior to the students' senior year. Students who meet the readiness standards are exempt from additional placement testing after they are admitted to CSU. Students who do not meet the standards are guided to further instructional and diagnostic assistance in the twelfth grade. For example, the diagnostic assistance includes courses and online tutorials; students can access the CSU Diagnostic Writing Service online and use materials from the Mathematics Diagnostic Testing Project.[26] In addition, K–12 and postsecondary educators have developed a twelfth-grade expository reading and writing course that high schools may pilot and adopt to help students advance their skills in English. The course is aligned with California's content standards; it is geared toward preparing students for college-level English; and it focuses on analytical, expository, and argumentative reading and writing.[27]

In spring 2004, testing for the Early Assessment Program was available in all California high schools. Out of approximately 386,000 eligible students, about 153,000 took the English language arts test. Based on the results, 22 percent of these students were exempted from taking placement tests at CSU. In math, out of approximately 157,000 eligible students, 115,000 took the test and 55 percent of these students were exempted.[28]

CSU "Lessons Learned" from the Early Assessment Program

State-level leadership and policy direction are needed to ensure that the same college-readiness signals are given to all high schools in a state, and that college-readiness standards and assessments are aligned with K–12 standards and assessments.

Public postsecondary and K–12 education systems must adopt the college-readiness standards.

Include all open-door and broad-access postsecondary institutions, since they have the potential to send the strongest, clearest signals about college readiness.

Emphasize policies and standards for placement into college-level courses, not admission to college.

Focus college-readiness standards on skills, such as reading, writing, and mathematics.

---

26. Ibid.
27. http://www.calstate.edu/eap/.
28. Spence, "Early Assessment Academic Preparation Initiative."

Define threshold performance levels and focus on a workable set of core skills.

Align the college-readiness standards and assessments with statewide high school standards and assessments, and evaluate the match between the sets, realigning if necessary. Do not rely on surrogate tests.

State high school assessments should include all of the college-readiness standards and range high enough in difficulty to indicate whether or not students have mastered the standards. High stakes tests are probably not suitable because the performance levels are too low and the tests might contribute to high school dropout rates. Comprehensive tests or end-of-course tests are better candidates.

Embed the college-readiness standards into curricula and assessments for grades 8 to 12. This includes teacher pre-service and in-service opportunities.

Source: David Spence, "Development of State College Readiness: School-Based Standards and Assessments," presentation at State Policy Dimensions for K–16 Reform, Wingspread Conference Center, September 12, 2005.

There are many anticipated benefits to the Early Assessment Program. For the first time, a large-scale, statewide program is providing students with information about their level of preparedness for college. If the program succeeds, students who participate will have the information and support to improve their academic readiness during their senior year in high school, and CSU will in turn have enrollees who will need fewer remedial classes and will graduate more quickly. The data generated will enable educators from both K–12 and postsecondary education to track student progress from high school through the CSU system—and thereby be in a better position to improve the alignment of course work and assessments between high school and college.[29]

Even though the statewide scope of this work is promising, its impact on California's public schools will be limited because the state's community college system, which enrolls about two-thirds of the college students in the state, has not participated in its development or implementation. Community colleges in Los Angeles, however, have decided to pilot the use of the Early Assessment Program for their campuses.

State Finance

States Should Develop Financial Incentives and Support to Stimulate K–12 and Postsecondary Education to Collaborate to Improve College Readiness and Success.

As well as requiring public education systems to align their assessments and course work, states need to create budget and finance incentives that can stimulate

29. Ibid.

increased collaboration between K–12 and postsecondary education to improve student achievement across the systems. Creating such incentives will require state legislative committees that oversee the budget processes for K–12 and higher education to work more closely together to find common goals in advancing college readiness and success. Currently, most states maintain separate legislative committee structures governing K–12 and postsecondary education. To the extent that these legislative oversight functions remain isolated from each other, they can and often do perpetuate the divide between schools and college systems.

No state has fully aligned its budget, its financial aid, and its other policies to provide incentives for K–12 and postsecondary education to support college readiness. However, several states have taken steps to provide such incentives in some areas, ranging from redesigning state budget processes for public education systems to, on a much smaller scale, providing incentives for dual enrollment. Two promising ambitious examples are summarized below: Oregon is exploring the development of an integrated K–20 finance model; Indiana is using a financial aid program to increase and broaden access to college-preparatory classes.

Oregon's K–20 Finance Model

In Oregon, the state political leadership has established expectations for improvement in how K–12 and postsecondary education collaborate to advance student success. For example, the governor has set concrete goals in the areas of high school graduation, college completion, and system delivery. In addition, the Joint Boards—comprised of members from the State Board of Education and the State Board of Higher Education—has recommended the following three infrastructure redesigns:

- a unified education delivery system with curriculum aligned so that exit standards from one sector equal entrance standards to the next;

- a unified data system that can track students across the continuum and by institution; and

- a unified, transparent budget that connects all education sectors.[30]

The Oregon Business Council has taken the lead in developing an integrated statewide budget and finance model that would span from preschool to graduate school. According to Duncan Wyse, president of the Oregon Business Council, the state's public education system, as in most states, "is composed of distinct sectors, budgeted and governed separately. There are no consistent [high school]

---

30. Duncan Wyse, "Oregon Public Education: A 'System' in Need of Direction (And Why the Budget Is the Key Tool)," presentation at State Policy Dimensions for K–16 Reform, Wingspread Conference Center, September 13, 2005.

exit and [postsecondary] entrance standards for students. Student movement through the system is organized by time rather than by achievement."[31]

In developing the model, the Business Council analyzed the 2002-03 expenditures by K–12 and postsecondary education as though they derived from one budget. The council found that the level of state investment per student varied by grade and degree, with community colleges receiving the least state funding and special education in K–12 schools receiving the most.[32] In addition, since the 1990 passage of Oregon's ballot measure establishing limits on property taxes, state investment in pre-K programs, middle school education, K–12 special education, and community college developmental education has increased. State investment in all other educational areas—elementary and high school education; community college lower-division education and professional training; and Oregon University System lower-division, upper-division, graduate, and professional education—decreased.[33]

The Business Council consequently recommended that Oregon adopt a reform plan to coordinate governance, budgeting, and management of education from preschool to graduate school. The council proposed that budgets would be based on per-student costs per service; outcomes would be established for every educational level and service; school spending would be more transparent; and aggregate student performance for every program and at every institution would be publicly reported. The governor, the legislature, and the Joint Boards would set performance expectations and priorities for the budget, create teams to work on efficiencies and delivery improvements in high-impact areas, and set forth a two- or three-biennium plan to accomplish the work. Through the Joint Boards, the governor would lead policy discussions and assign teams to address improvements in areas such as high school redesign, high school and lower-division alignment, policies for tuition and need-based aid for public and private institutions, K–12 transportation, special education, and English as a second language.[34]

The Oregon Business Council has acknowledged that there are many hurdles to overcome in implementing this reform plan. For example, the state's budget and accounting systems are not adequate to collect and report comparable per-student costs by service across institutions, and developing this capacity would require significant legislative and public support. In addition, these

---

31. Duncan Wyse, "Governing the Enterprise Pre-K–20: Oregon Is Poised to Adopt a New Vision and a New Structure to Meet 21st-Century Demands for More and Better Education," presentation to the Oregon Business Council, Portland, Oregon, 2005.

32. Ibid.

33. Wyse, "Oregon Public Education: A 'System' in Need of Direction."

34. Ibid.

transformations would take longer than any single governor's term; sustaining reforms across administrations is difficult. Finally, since some stakeholders are likely to perceive the changes as threatening, there could be political setbacks along the way as people resist the reforms.[35]

According to the Business Council, if Oregon succeeds in implementing this model, the state should be able to reduce financial inefficiencies, target resources more strategically, improve student achievement across every educational level, and provide a more transparent and unified system of financing. The council has suggested that the benefits would also include more informed decisions for policy and educational leaders, transparency of tax dollar use, the creation of opportunities for broad redesign and reinvention, and increases in program effectiveness by focusing on service quality and continuous improvement.[36]

Indiana's Twenty-first Century Scholars Program

State financial aid, a traditional means for broadening access to college, can also be used to leverage college-readiness reforms. Indiana's Twenty-first Century Scholars Program is a national model in both broadening access to college and improving college readiness. Initiated in 1990, the program was the first state financial aid program to promise the future payment of college tuition for middle school students who qualify for the federal free and reduced-price lunch program. The Scholars Program targets low-income students in the eighth grade and requires each participating student to complete a pledge to finish high school, maintain at least a C grade point average, remain drug- and alcohol-free, apply for college and financial aid, and enroll in an Indiana postsecondary institution within two years of completing high school. In return, Indiana: (1) encourages the Scholars to pursue a college-preparatory curriculum; (2) provides support services to them; and (3) for those who fulfill the pledge, pays their tuition and fees (after other financial aid awards) at a public institution in Indiana (or contributes a similar portion for tuition at an independent college).[37] The program pays for 80 percent of the approved tuition and fees for students completing a regular high school diploma; 90 percent of tuition and fees for students completing a more rigorous high school diploma, called a core 40 diploma; and 100 percent of tuition and fees for students completing the most rigorous diploma, the academic

---

35. Ibid.

36. Ibid.

37. Edward St. John, Jacob Gross, Glenda Musoba, and Anna Chung, *A Step Toward College Success: Assessing Attainment Among Indiana's Twenty-first Century Scholars* (Indianapolis: Lumina Foundation for Education, 2005), http://www.luminafoundation.org/publications/CollegeSuccess.pdf.

honors diploma. Through these incentives, the program sends clear signals to students regarding academic preparation for college.[38]

Since the Scholars Program targets low-income students, the majority of students who receive the awards already qualify for some level of state financial aid. As a result, the program's award amounts are relatively modest.[39] In contrast, the Georgia HOPE Scholarship provides financial aid to students who earn a B or better in the college-preparatory track, regardless of financial need. As with Indiana's Scholars Program, the HOPE Scholarship provides clear signals to students about the importance of college readiness. Because HOPE is not tied to financial need, however, it is expensive for the state and has been criticized for its failure to target low-income students.

The Scholars Program is increasing enrollment in rigorous preparatory curricula in high school and enrollment in colleges and universities. The percentage of traditionally underserved students taking college-preparatory curricula in high school has increased, as has the percentage of all students taking such courses. In 1993-94, 12 percent of Indiana's high school graduates earned an academic honors diploma, 87 percent earned a regular diploma, and 1 percent were in the "other" category. In 2003-04, 29 percent earned an academic honors diploma, 36 percent earned a core 40 diploma, and 35 percent earned a regular diploma. Although gaps in educational attainment by race and ethnicity persist, they are narrowing, and the performance of each racial and ethnic group is improving. For example, in 1998, 23 percent of African American, 29 percent of Hispanic, 45 percent of white, and 36 percent of multiracial high school graduates earned a core 40 diploma. In 2004, those percentages increased to 47 percent, 51 percent, 67 percent, and 66 percent, respectively.[40]

In addition, the percentage of students enrolling in postsecondary education has risen. From 1994 to 2002, the percentage of Indiana's high school graduates who enrolled in college right after high school increased from 50 percent to 62 percent, raising the state's rank on this measure from 34th to 10th in the nation. In terms of raw numbers, in 1988 Indiana had 69,004 high school graduates and 30,905 college freshmen. In 2002, it had 60,943 high school graduates and 38,023 college freshmen.[41]

A report from the Lumina Foundation found that the Scholars Program is encouraging more low-income students to enroll in postsecondary education.

---

38. Phone conversation with Dennis Obergfell, State Student Assistance Commission, Aug. 2, 2005.

39. St. John, Gross, Musoba, and Chung, *A Step Toward College Success.*

40. Stanley Jones, "Access to Higher Education in Indiana," presentation at State Policy Dimensions for K–16 Reform, Wingspread Conference Center, September 12, 2005.

41. Ibid.

The report also found that the program is improving persistence and completion rates for students earning two-year college degrees. The Lumina report concludes that "state policy can affect the curricula that students actually complete, which, in turn, can influence their college success."[42]

As states seek to develop their own budget or financial incentives to improve college readiness and success, they need to be mindful of unintended effects of such efforts. For example, many state legislators, concerned about the high costs of college, may be interested in creating incentives to improve certificate- or degree-completion rates at state colleges or universities. Some states, for example, have provided postsecondary institutions with additional funds for each student who graduates. Such incentives do not always succeed, however, because many institutions can improve their graduation rates by raising their admissions requirements in ways that have the effect of reducing access to college statewide. States might consider developing programs similar to Indiana's Scholars Program, which addresses financial need and college readiness, thereby broadening access to college while also improving students' abilities to perform at higher levels.

Statewide Data Systems
**States Should Develop the Capacity to Track Students
Across Educational Institutions Statewide.**

A third important element in college-readiness reform is the development of statewide databases that can track student progress across educational institutions. A robust statewide data system is needed to determine the effectiveness of programs and reforms in improving student achievement.

Currently, the data derived from state information systems are generally more useful for supporting budget allocations to institutions than for examining student progress across multiple institutions. At the K–12 level, most state databases cannot track students who leave one school district and enroll in another. Many cannot accurately determine the percentage of students graduating from high school each year. State databases are even more deficient in examining student transitions from high school to college; most states have data systems that stop at grade 12 and others that begin anew at grade 13, with little or no connection between them. As a consequence, these states do not have adequate information to address the effectiveness of K–12 reforms in improving student performance in college.

As states seek to align and expand their information systems across K–12 and postsecondary education, they need to fully understand the relationship between

---

42. St. John, Gross, Musoba, and Chung, *A Step Toward College Success.*

student readiness in high school and student success in college. Currently, 18 states do not even collect data on the courses taken by high school students. In most states, it is not currently possible to identify and analyze completion rates for students who enter college from the workforce, for students who attend part-time, and for students who attend multiple institutions. In short, without databases that connect educational institutions, it is difficult—if not impossible— to assess needs accurately, identify where the most substantial problems are, and design appropriate interventions.

In tracking student progress across educational institutions and systems, state information systems need to standardize and report data on high school academic courses and assessments, high school graduation, college and work readiness, transitions between high school and college, transfers between colleges, student progress while in college, and completion of postsecondary education and training programs. For example, the databases should be designed to answer questions related to college readiness:

- How do students who take college-preparatory courses in high school perform in postsecondary education?

- How do students who pass (or earn a proficient score on) state assessments perform in college?

- Considering those students who require remediation in college, what percentage took a college-preparatory curriculum in high school?

- Given their students' performance in college, how can high schools strengthen their curricula and instruction to improve student readiness for college?

Most states have been developing better ways to track student achievement, and a few have been working to connect their information systems for K–12 and postsecondary education. Florida's linked data systems represent one of the more ambitious efforts to connect the two education systems through better data gathering.

Florida's Linked Data Systems

Florida has linked two data collection systems in order to track student progress through the state's education systems, their participation in other public systems, and their later status in the workforce: the Data Warehouse, and the Florida Education and Training Placement Information Program. In integrating the data systems, Florida is developing common standards, procedures, and quality assurance; eliminating duplicated functions and services; providing for improved accountability and public reporting; and establishing longitudinal reporting about the status and performance of students and other public program participants.

The Data Warehouse combines longitudinal student data from public schools, community colleges and technical centers, and the university system. Florida has had a history of gathering data across educational institutions on an ad hoc basis, but over the past several years the State Department of Education has worked to formally connect all public databases using common student identifiers. The Data Warehouse is managed by the Information and Accountability Division of the Office of K–20 Education. The warehouse includes data on K–12 students; adult, vocational, and associate programs in community and technical colleges; public university, baccalaureate, master's, doctorate, and professional programs in four-year, in-state universities; assessment systems, financial aid, teacher certification, and facilities across the K–20 spectrum; and employment and continuing education outcomes. The warehouse includes the following data categories: individual students (demographics, enrollment, courses, test scores, financial aid, awards, and employment); educational curricula; staff information; program costs; and workforce information.[43]

The Florida Education and Training Placement Information Program follows students when they leave any level of schooling (at the high school level or above), whether they continue their education, participate in a training program (for example, vocational rehabilitation), receive public assistance, enter a correctional facility, or earn an occupational licensure. The program also contains data about whether a former student is employed or unemployed. The program integrates data from a variety of state and federal agencies, including Florida's Agency for Workforce Innovation, Department of Children and Families, Department of Corrections, and Department of Education; and the federal government's Department of Defense, Office of Personnel Management, and United States Postal Service.[44]

Because of its integrated data systems, Florida can track students over time and across educational institutions, enabling state staff, researchers, and others to answer many questions about the effectiveness of education at various levels.

Florida's Linked Data Systems Enable the State to:

Track students across K–12 schools and districts.

Analyze the impact of specific policies (for example, the participation of students in the Bright Futures Scholarship Program or their completion of Algebra I) to understand the policies' impact on students' future educational attainment and earnings.

Examine student performance on the high stakes test and determine the test's validity in relation to student activities in the ensuing years.

---

43. http://edwapp.doe.state.fl.us/doe/EDW_Facts.htm.
44. Phone conversation with Jay J. Pfeiffer, Florida Department of Education, January 27, 2006.

Track students beyond the K 12 system, including students who drop out, to see the overall impact of their experiences in school.

Track students who were successful on state exams—and those who were not—in order to examine the characteristics of teachers who appear to be successful (at the aggregate level).

Examine longitudinal data for students who complete high school in various ways (for example, through obtaining a standard diploma, a special certificate, or a certificate of completion), their success in postsecondary education, and their employment status.

Determine former high school students' earnings based on their highest level of education attained: high school dropout, high school diploma, adult diploma, vocational, college credit vocational, associate degree, bachelor's degree, or more than a bachelor's degree.

Compare how different student groups exited high school. In 1996, for example, 89,461 students earned a standard diploma; 2,329 earned a special diploma; 247 earned a special certificate; and 31,775 dropped out. For students with disabilities, those figures were 4,653; 2,262; 224; and 5,166, respectively.

Source: Jay J. Pfeiffer, Assistant Deputy Commissioner of Accountability, Research, and Measurement, Florida Department of Education, "Florida's Education Pipeline: ESE Students with Standard High School Diplomas," presentation to the Florida Legislature, January 16, 2006.

Accountability
States Should Publicly Report on Student Progress and Success from High School Through Postsecondary Education.

To be effective in improving college readiness, states should establish student achievement objectives that require the education systems to collaborate to achieve them. Schools, colleges, and universities should be held accountable for improving student performance from high school to college completion.

The public reporting of student progress and achievement across educational levels is crucial to the development of collaborative efforts to advance student-readiness reforms. Requiring education institutions to report data to state departments of education, however, will not suffice in making the systems more accountable for student achievement. States need to work with educational leaders to develop clear student achievement targets that will require K–12 and postsecondary systems to achieve them jointly. Ultimately, the primary outcomes for state accountability systems should become the percentage of the young population completing high school prepared for college (college readiness), the percentage enrolling in college (participation and access), the percentage staying in college (persistence), and the percentage graduating (completion). In addition, key indicators at various stages can include, for example, high school graduation and transfers from community colleges to four-year institutions.

Although no state has instituted a comprehensive accountability system focused on improving college readiness and success, several states have developed accountability elements linking K–12 and higher education. Kentucky's accountability system for postsecondary education offers a promising example.

Kentucky's Accountability System for Postsecondary Education

In 1997, the Kentucky Legislature passed the Postsecondary Education Improvement Act of 1997 (House Bill 1). In addition to establishing goals for the state's system of postsecondary education, the legislation charged the Council on Postsecondary Education with developing an accountability system to "ensure institutions' compliance with the strategic plan and to measure: educational quality and student progress in the postsecondary education system, research and service opportunities, and use of resources by institutions."[45] To address this charge, the council developed a public agenda focusing on accountability, degree completion, and affordability of postsecondary and adult education through 2010.

Kentucky's Goals for Postsecondary Education

Provide an integrated system of postsecondary education to enhance job opportunities and the quality of life for Kentucky's residents.

Raise the level of national recognition for the state's flagship universities.

Promote cooperation among postsecondary institutions in order to increase access.

Design a community and technical college system to improve access.

Increase the efficiency, responsiveness, quality, and quantity of postsecondary education services.

Source: http://cpe.ky.gov/NR/rdonlyrcs/04F25118-4FBB-4C8A-8D1B-4197EA4CEAEA/0/ SummaryHB1_20050401.pdf.

The state's accountability system was developed around the following key questions:

• Are more Kentuckians ready for postsecondary education?

• Is Kentucky postsecondary education affordable to its citizens?

• Do more Kentuckians have certificates and degrees?

---

45. http://cpe.ky.gov/NR/rdonlyres/04F25118-4FBB-4C8A-8D1B-4197EA4CEAEA/0/ SummaryHB1_20050401.pdf.

- Are college graduates prepared for life and work in Kentucky?

- Are Kentucky's people, communities, and economy benefiting?[46]

The council developed state-level indicators for each question and outlined related benefits. For example, to answer the first question regarding college readiness, the council has required that the following data be collected:

- K–12 student achievement (average ACT);

- the percentage of high school students scoring a three or higher on Advanced Placement Program® Exams;

- the percentage of incoming Kentucky high school graduates not requiring remediation in math and English; and

- the number of Kentuckians earning general equivalency diplomas (GEDs).[47]

By including indicators for college readiness in its accountability system for postsecondary education, Kentucky has set high expectations for collaborative work between K–12 schools and colleges and universities to improve student achievement. There is evidence that the reform efforts may be improving student success in college.

Indicators of Kentucky's Improvements in Postsecondary Education

Undergraduate student enrollment increased from 160,926 in 1998 to 205,832 in 2005.

By 2004, 82 percent of adults age 25 or older had a high school diploma or a GED, up from 78 percent in 1998.

In 2004 at public universities, 44 percent of students graduated within six years of enrolling in college, up from 37 percent in 1998.

After the development of the Kentucky Community and Technical College System, enrollment grew from 52,201 in 2000 to 81,990 in 2004.

The Research Challenge Trust Fund spent $350 million on postsecondary education from 1997 to 2003, enabling the University of Kentucky and the University of Louisville to hire dozens of new professors.

Source: http://www.highereducation.org/crosstalk/ct0405/news0405-kentucky.shtml.

---

46. http://cpe.ky.gov/planning/5Qs/default.htm.

47. http://cpe.ky.gov/NR/rdonlyres/E88C6729-09CA-4DF4-BB34-CD6C34CBDD37/0/StateKI_Summary.pdf.

The Challenges Ahead

The policies recommended in this essay do not exhaust the range of steps that states may need to consider. For example, K–16 governance commissions can assist in initiating and maintaining state action in the four policy areas. Creating these entities, however, is not sufficient in itself. In some cases, statewide K–16 bodies have become little more than discussion forums—deflecting energy from policy changes and sometimes even exacerbating tensions between K–12 and postsecondary leaders. To be effective, K–16 commissions should be charged with substantive responsibilities in such areas as alignment and coordinating the development of data and accountability systems; they should be provided the requisite resources; they should have sufficient influence and authority to make real change; and they should be held accountable for their own performance.

Improving collaboration among state agencies and among state legislative committees can also be important in developing effective state policies for K–16, particularly since most states have created regulatory and governing frameworks that perpetuate the divide between K–12 and postsecondary education. In addition, adopting legislation that outlines elements of K–16 reform appears to be useful in creating the conditions for change, but is not sufficient in itself. (For example, Georgia passed legislation mandating that a statewide P–16 council meet on a regular basis. The council made progress under former Governor Roy Barnes but has not met under Governor Sonny Perdue.)

Engaging in reforms suggested by this essay necessarily involves political as well as educational challenges. States may struggle with how to involve the governor or the appropriate legislative committees, and how to sustain the reforms after leaders leave office. Each state's responses to these challenges will be unique, tempered by historical context, political culture, and the educational and other resources that are available. Nonetheless, no state's political or educational context creates insurmountable hurdles to this agenda. Challenges await, but the appropriate policy levers are available to each state, and each state must determine how best to implement them.

Conclusion

In many ways, the United States produces the college outcomes that its systems of education were designed to produce. Its K–12 system was developed to provide education to everyone; its college and university system was developed when only a few were expected to attend college. Today, the vast majority of high school students aspire to attend college, but only about half of the students who enroll in college are prepared for college-level academic work. And less than 40 percent of the young workforce (ages 25 to 34) has a postsecondary degree.[48] The era of providing postsecondary education for only a small group of students is over; yet our state educational policies remain locked in a former era.

As the entities that perform the major funding and policy-setting functions for education, states are in the unique position to claim common ground between K–12 and postsecondary education. This essay identifies four state policy dimensions to advance college readiness and success: the alignment of course work and assessments, state finance, statewide data systems, and accountability. By developing and coordinating their policies in each of these areas, states can require and assist schools, colleges, and universities in working together toward a common goal—to significantly increase the number of students graduating from high school and completing college-level education and training—and thereby advance the educational achievement of millions of young Americans.

---

48. Kelly, *As America Becomes More Diverse.*

Conclusion: Making Opportunity Real

Michael S. McPherson and Morton Owen Schapiro

The sources of unequal college opportunity in the United States run deep. The essays in this volume have approached the problem of unequal access to college from a variety of perspectives and have shed light on the opportunities and challenges facing those who would act to improve college access and success for the disadvantaged.

Finding effective ways to act is a matter of growing urgency and importance. There is every reason to think that success in higher education will become continually more critical for individual success in our economy and society. And a well-educated populace seems indispensable for a healthy and flourishing society in this new century, both in economic and in civic terms. For Americans to tolerate an educational system that poorly serves a significant segment of the population—especially a segment disproportionately composed of the children of the economically disadvantaged and of persons of color—is morally unacceptable in its own right, and it threatens to become a source of larger social failures in the decades ahead.

One of the big challenges to acting effectively is our knowledge that educational failures at any one life stage can often be traced back to earlier stages, all the way back to preschool and to home and community life in the earliest years. It is tempting then to argue that, for example, rather than "wasting time" on remediation in college, we should "fix" the high schools and get it right the first time, and likewise that the high schools can't do much if their students have not learned to read and calculate in elementary school, and so on. The fundamentally sound idea of success building on success has led James Heckman and a variety of other analysts to argue, quite persuasively, for the importance of investments in high-quality day care and preschool education.[1] It's possible abstractly to imagine a sort of perfectly ordered world in which great preschools were followed by strong elementary schools, then high schools, and on to excellent colleges from which in 20 or 25 years a much better and more equally educated generation of young adults would emerge. Just start with the next generation of newborns and work from there.

---

1. James Heckman, "Catch 'em Young," *Wall Street Journal* (January 10, 2006): A14.

Yet, while it is a good idea to keep that kind of long-run vision before us as we go about the current business of reform, it is obviously unacceptable to simply write off all the young people living right now for whom improved preschool simply comes too late. Even if that were somehow tolerable, a second problem bedevils this approach as well. There is considerable evidence that one of the human activities that improves with better education is parenting, and there is evidence that the quality and character of home life in a child's early years importantly influence his or her later educational success. Thus investing now in the education of future parents should be part of any comprehensive long-run strategy for improving educational opportunity and outcomes in future generations. After Bill Bowen and Derek Bok published their powerful study, *The Shape of the River*,[2] showing the positive effects of affirmative action in college admissions, some critics said that the real challenge was to address the failings of the public schools, not make up for those failings through affirmative action in college. As Bill Bowen said at the time: "We do not have to choose; we have two hands."

So, rather than waiting for education reform at earlier ages to somehow overcome inequalities, we think that colleges, and those who shape government policies toward college education, need to find effective ways to act now in the face of the very large inequalities in college access and opportunity they currently face.

A very big message that emerges from the essays in this volume is that what colleges can reasonably do depends very heavily on how they are situated. While a minority of college students attend colleges and universities that select enrollees from a broad pool of applicants, the majority are at places where all or most of the students who apply are admitted. It is the former group that can practice racial affirmative action in admissions and may also consider "economic" affirmative action—the "thumb on the scale" advocated in *Equity and Excellence in American Higher Education*.[3] Even within that selective group only a relative handful are likely to have adequate resources to expand their admission of low-income applicants significantly. (Even among selective colleges, the majority turn down some otherwise qualified applicants because the colleges want to avoid the financial aid costs of their enrollment.)

It is our strong sense that those selective colleges and universities with the capacity to enroll more low-income students should do so, a step made all the more important by the fact that these institutions are widely seen as America's

---

2. William G. Bowen and Derek C. Bok, *The Shape of the River: Long-Term Consequences of Considering Race in College and University Admissions* (Princeton, N.J.: Princeton University Press, 1998).

3. William G. Bowen, Martin A. Kurzweil, and Eugene M. Tobin, *Equity and Excellence in American Higher Education* (Charlottesville, Va.: University of Virginia Press, 2005).

higher education leaders. Hill and Winston's essay provides evidence that there is a large pool of low-income students who have the level of academic preparation needed for success at these places.

We do not at all wish to imply that those institutions that lack the resources or the selectivity to practice "economic affirmative action" are "off the hook" in regard to addressing the needs of low-income students. Indeed, it is at these less affluent and less selective colleges and universities that most low-income students can be found. A major contribution these institutions can make is to find ways to help more of their disadvantaged students make a success of their college efforts. We know that low-income students who start college are less likely than others to complete their studies. As Mike Nettles and Catherine Millett discuss in their contribution, this outcome is caused by some combination of inadequate academic preparation, financial shortfalls, and personal and cultural difficulties that colleges need to understand better and devise more effective ways to address. There is also a need to understand when and how remediation works for students in college and how to make it work better.[4]

Colleges should also be "on the hook" for working more effectively with secondary school systems to make sure that schools understand and communicate to their students what kind of preparation is needed for college success. As Callan et al. argue in their essay, and as Rosenbaum has argued elsewhere,[5] what it takes to graduate from high school or to be admitted to college is only distantly related to the kind of preparation needed to succeed in a college environment. Aligning standards and then, importantly, offering educational programs that will enable students to meet those standards are much needed.

We think the voices in this volume, including those of the campus leaders reported on by David Breneman, offer heartening evidence that at least a good many colleges take the problem of improving low-income access and success seriously and want to devise ways to address the challenges they face. At the same time, there are severe limits on what individual colleges, acting separately, can do to address the underlying problems. Some such challenges can be tackled by colleges themselves acting collectively through their associations and consortia. Collective efforts to communicate with high school students and their families about preparing for college and about how to pay for it, like the American Council

---

4. Eric Bettinger and Bridget Terry Long, "The Role of Institutional Responses to Reduce Inequalities in College Outcomes: Remediation in Higher Education," in *Economic Inequality and Higher Education: Access, Persistence, and Success*, edited by S. Dickert-Conlin and R. Rubenstein (New York: Russell Sage Foundation, forthcoming).

5. James E. Rosenbaum, *Beyond College for All: Career Paths for the Forgotten Half*, American Sociological Association's Rose Series in Sociology (New York: Russell Sage Foundation, 2001).

on Education's "College Is Possible" campaign, are examples. Some observers have argued that there is potential for making these efforts substantially more effective by basing them on a more systematic study of what families know and how they learn about colleges.[6] It would also be desirable for colleges to do more to cooperate in putting their financial aid dollars where they would do the most good, although that probably cannot be done without affording the colleges some protection from antitrust prosecution.

A major constraint on what both individual colleges and cooperating groups of colleges can do about low-income access is money. The influence of family resources on college-going decisions is exerted through multiple channels. Possibly the biggest influence is through the fact that families with less income and wealth are not able to devote as many educational resources to their children from an early age as more affluent families can, with the result that their children are on average less well prepared academically for college. Low-income families are also often less well equipped to navigate the complex and disjointed systems by which financial aid for college is provided, even as they are more dependent on its assistance.

But there is also reason to believe that money still matters in college access in the straightforward sense that low-income families struggle to pay the bills. Studies that attempt to control for the influence of factors like academic preparation and parental education still find that money matters significantly in influencing college attendance.[7] Even James Heckman, who thinks the direct influence of access to financing on college enrollment is often exaggerated, suggests that as many as 8 percent of high school graduates may face credit constraints in attending college.[8] Federal loan limits for undergraduates have not been raised in over a decade, and the value of the maximum Pell Grant is substantially lower now as a fraction of college tuition than it was in the mid-1970s. Particularly for students whose best educational option is a four-year college or university away from home, financial constraints can be very real. Moreover, it is very hard, given

---

6. David S. Mundel and Ann S. Coles. "An exploration of what we know about the formation and impact of perceptions of college prices, student aid, and the affordability of college-going and a prospectus for future research" Summary Project Report. The Education Research Institute, Boston, MA. (2004), http://www.teri.org/research-studies/financial-aid-impact.asp.

7. David T. Ellwood and Thomas J. Kane, "Who Is Getting a College Education? Family Background and the Growing Gaps in Enrollment," in *Securing the Future: Investing in Children from Birth to College*, The Ford Foundation Series on Asset Building, edited by S. Danziger and J. Waldfogel (New York: Russell Sage Foundation, 2000), 283–324.

8. Pedro Carneiro and James Heckman, "The Evidence on Credit Constraints in Postsecondary Schooling" *Economic Journal* 112, No. 482 (October, 2002): 705–734.

the way financial aid works now, for a family to look ahead when their child is 10 or 13 years old and see with any clarity how college will be paid for. This fact can be a serious discouragement to making the key choices in middle school and high school that will make success in college feasible.

These are not problems that colleges and universities, public or private, can overcome on their own. They must be addressed through public policy, principally at state and federal levels. Some of what is needed might be accomplished through more purposeful use of existing public resources. A significant fraction of state government subsidies, for example, goes to reduce the tuition paid by affluent families who could readily pay more. But there is also a case for expanding federal and state commitments to helping low-income people finance their college education.

This doesn't have to mean simply putting more money into existing programs like Pell. There is much to be said for exploring innovative policies that will involve a simpler, more understandable delivery of benefits, that will encourage advance planning and solid academic preparation in high school, and that will have a broader political base than the narrowly targeted Pell program.

The good news is that there is plenty of work to go around. Well-endowed selective colleges and universities can exert a leading role by expanding their representation of disadvantaged students. The broad-access institutions that now enroll most low-income students can develop programs to foster their success in college and work with high schools to send clearer messages about what is needed for academic success in college. And policymakers in state and federal governments can work to use existing resources more effectively while also making commitments to expanded and improved programs to make a good college experience a realistic option for all who qualify. Do what you can with what you have where you are.

Acknowledgments

Alan Heaps and his colleagues at the College Board have been a joy to work with as we have brought this volume to press. We are grateful to Gaston Caperton, president of the College Board, for his vision in supporting our efforts to bring the message of this book to the secondary and postsecondary leaders who make up the College Board.

This project has been the work of many hands, just as, we expect, tackling the problems addressed in this volume will necessarily be. Our greatest debt is to Bill Bowen, whose encouragement, support, and intellectual leadership have proved invaluable to us. We have immensely enjoyed Humphrey Doermann's partnership in this enterprise. His balanced judgment, personal modesty, and quiet efficiency have made this a much more successful book (if indeed it would even have become a book without his help). David Breneman gave generously of his time and advice in bringing this project to fruition. We are grateful as well to Sandy Baum for sharing her wide knowledge both about the facts and about purpose and policy. Doris Fischer provided gracious, careful management of manuscript details and conference arrangements described below.

Much of the analysis presented here was prepared initially for a conference on college accessibility sponsored by the Spencer Foundation and Macalester College, with financial assistance from the Andrew W. Mellon Foundation, and held June 21–22, 2005, at Oak Brook, Illinois. The conference was attended by 85 scholars, college and university leaders, and observers of U.S. postsecondary education. Essays in this book are written by presenters at the conference. The conference series is supported by the Mellon Foundation and has been held either at Macalester College, Saint Paul, or under Spencer Foundation auspices in the Chicago area. The 2005 conference was the fourth in this series of biennial meetings concerning major issues in higher education.

Michael S. McPherson
Morton Owen Schapiro
May 2006

Contributing Authors

William G. Bowen is president of the Andrew W. Mellon Foundation in New York. Previously, he was president of Princeton University. Bowen is a prolific author on the economics and governance of higher education. His recent major works include *Equity and Excellence in American Higher Education* (University of Virginia Press, 2005) with Martin A. Kurzweil and Eugene M. Tobin and *The Shape of the River: Long-Term Consequences of Considering Race in College and University Admissions* (Princeton University Press, 1998) with Derek Bok.

David W. Breneman is university professor and dean of the Curry School of Education at the University of Virginia in Charlottesville. Breneman is an economist and authority on the economics of higher education. His prior appointments include visiting professor at the Harvard Graduate School of Education and president of Kalamazoo College. He is the author of *Liberal Arts Colleges: Thriving, Surviving, or Endangered?* (The Brookings Institution, 1994).

Patrick M. Callan is president of the National Center for Public Policy and Higher Education. He has previously served as executive director of the California Higher Education Policy Center, the California Postsecondary Education Commission, the Washington State Council for Postsecondary Education, and the Montana Commission on Postsecondary Education; and as vice president of the Education Commission of the States (ECS).

Joni E. Finney is vice president of the National Center for Public Policy and Higher Education. Finney oversees the research, communication, and administration of the National Center. Prior to her position at the National Center, she held senior policy positions with the California Higher Education Policy Center, the Education Commission of the States, the Pennsylvania State University, and the University of Southern Colorado.

Catharine B. Hill is the recently elected president of Vassar College in Poughkeepsie, New York. Previously, she was provost of Williams College and John J. Gibson Professor of Economics. Her co-authored contribution to this volume is part of a several years collaboration with Gordon C. Winston at Williams College on issues of access and affordability in higher education.

Michael W. Kirst is professor of education at Stanford University and former president of the California State Board of Education. Before joining the Stanford University faculty, Kirst held several positions with the federal government, including staff director of the U.S. Senate Subcommittee on Manpower, Employment, and Poverty, and director of program planning and evaluation for the Bureau of Elementary and Secondary Education in the former U.S. Office of Education. He was the principal investigator for Stanford University's Bridge Project and is co-author of *Betraying the College Dream* (Stanford University, 2003) and *From High School to College: Improving Opportunities for Success in Postsecondary Education* (Jossey-Bass, 2004).

Alan B. Krueger is Bendheim Professor of Economics and Public Policy and director of the Princeton University Survey Research Center. He is the author of *Education Matters* (Edward Elgar Publishing, 2001) and writes a monthly column on economics for the *New York Times*. In this volume, he co-authors with Jesse Rothstein and Sarah Turner the essay that projects diversity for 25 years in selective colleges.

Michael S. McPherson is president of the Spencer Foundation in Chicago, and former president of Macalester College in Saint Paul, Minnesota. Much of his prior career was at Williams College, where he was a professor, chair of the Economics Department, and dean of faculty. McPherson collaborated with Morton Owen Schapiro in editing this volume, as he has in co-authoring other books and articles on college access.

Catherine M. Millett is a research scientist in the Policy Evaluation and Research Center at Educational Testing Service. Her research focuses on access, student performance and achievement, educational equity, and student financing for various population groups in the United States at the postsecondary educational level. One area of her current research is on the doctoral student experience. She is co-author with Michael Nettles of *Three Magic Letters: Getting to Ph.D.* (Johns Hopkins University Press), 2005.

Michael T. Nettles is senior vice president for Policy Evaluation and Research and holds the Edmund W. Gordon Chair for Policy Evaluation and Research at Educational Testing Service. Prior to this appointment, Nettles was professor of education at the University of Michigan and also served as the first executive director of the Frederick D. Patterson Research Institute at the United Negro College Fund. He is a frequent author and consultant on many topics, including equity, educational testing and assessment, and undergraduate student access and degree progress.

Jesse Rothstein is assistant professor of economics and public affairs at Princeton University and a faculty research fellow at the National Bureau of Economic Research. His recent research is on the economics of education, and he has written several papers on background factors affecting college performance.

Morton Owen Schapiro is professor of economics and president of Williams College. Most of his academic career has been at Williams College, except for the 1990s when he was chair of the Department of Economics at the University of Southern California and then dean of the College of Arts and Letters. He is a long-term collaborator with Michael S. McPherson on the economics of higher education, concentrating often on issues of college accessibility and U.S. student aid policy. McPherson and Schapiro are co-authors of *The Student Aid Game: Meeting Need and Rewarding Talent in American Higher Education* (Princeton University Press, 1998).

Jeffrey Tebbs is a research analyst in the Economics Studies Program at the Brookings Institution in Washington, D.C. Tebbs began this collaboration with Sarah Turner, describing the AccessUVa initiative, when he was an undergraduate student at the University of Virginia. His current research interests include the impact of early education on economic growth and access to postsecondary education.

Sarah Turner is associate professor of education and economics at the University of Virginia in Charlottesville and is a faculty research associate of the National Bureau of Economic Research. In this volume, Turner collaborated with Jesse Rothstein and Alan B. Krueger in a 25-year projection of diversity without affirmative action. Turner also is co-author with Jeffrey Tebbs of the description of the AccessUVa initiative.

Michael D. Usdan is a senior fellow at the Institute for Educational Leadership (IEL). He was president of IEL for 20 years. Before joining IEL, he was Connecticut's commissioner of higher education, and he served as president of the Merrill-Palmer Institute in Detroit.

Andrea Venezia is a senior policy analyst and project director at the National Center for Public Policy and Higher Education. Her work examines education policy, particularly as related to equity and the transition from K–12 to postsecondary education. Prior to joining the National Center, she directed Stanford University's Bridge Project and co-authored *Betraying the College Dream* (Stanford University, 2003) and *From High School to College: Improving Opportunities for Success in Postsecondary Education* (Jossey-Bass, 2004).

Gordon C. Winston is Orrin Sage Professor of Political Economy, Emeritus, and helped found the Project on the Economics of Higher Education at Williams College. He was provost of Williams College from 1988 to 1990 and twice served as chair of the Economics Department. Following his term as provost, Winston has focused on the economics of higher education. His contribution to this volume, collaborating with Catharine B. Hill, analyzes access to selective colleges by high-ability, low-income students.

Index